The Magic Keys

JOSEPH MURPHY'S GOLDEN LESSONS

The Magic Keys

Secrets to Success and Happiness

by Joseph Murphy

Author of *The Power of Your Subconscious Mind*

Edited by
Mitch Horowitz

MEDIA

MEDIA

Published 2022 by Gildan Media LLC
aka G&D Media
www.GandDmedia.com

The Collected Lectures of Dr. Joseph Murphy Copyright © 2004
Joseph Murphy Trust

THE MAGIC KEYS. Copyright © 2022 Joseph Murphy Trust. All rights
exclusively licensed by JMW Group Inc., jmwgroup@jmwgroup.net.

Front cover design by David Rheinhardt of Pyrographx

Interior design by Meghan Day Healey of Story Horse, LLC

Library of Congress Cataloging-in-Publication Data is available
upon request

ISBN 978-1-7225-0555-4

10   9   8   7   6   5   4   3   2   1

CONTENTS

PREFACE:
"A SURVIVING POINT OF VIEW"

"I have a surviving point of view.
I'm not interested in sinking or floating."

Joseph Murphy quotes these words from Virginia Graham (1912–1998), a television host and cancer survivor. For me, they form the centerpiece of this collection. I am not suggesting that everyone will have the same response to or experience with the ideas encountered in these collected pieces. But Graham's testimony, found in Murphy's essay "The Fourth Way to Pray," is one to live by.

What is your point of view on life? One of the misnomers about "positive thinking" is that it must result in the same kind of personality: rosy, ebullient, upbeat. I dissent from that. Positivity can take many forms—including deliberateness, persistence (what some call faith), and, as in Graham's case, "a surviving point of view." Novelist Charles Portis called it "true grit."

Whether or not you are traditionally religious, and I am not, the ideas, methods, and metaphysical truths in this book can inculcate you with a point of view of excellence, achievement, and ability. The ideas in this book are, in effect, a set of "magic keys," as alluded in its title, to entering and exercising your awareness of the greater laws and forces in which you play a part and which are felt upon and through you. This awareness itself is, in Murphy's phrase "the fourth way to pray."

The medium through which to contact these greater laws is your psyche—an amalgam of intellect and emotion. Years of comparative study and personal effort have persuaded me of a simple truth, which resounds in Murphy's work: thoughts are causative. In an ultimate sense, thoughts are the tissue of creation itself.

●   ●   ●

In this book Murphy writes that a way to glimpse and begin to exercise your greater possibilities is through prompt decision making. Decisions are often the product of intuition—an elusive trait that I believe results both from one's storehouse of information (never neglect that) and some degree of participation in nonlocal intelligence or a Higher Mind. The Ancient Greeks called this quality of mind *Nous*. The very term *genius*, in its original Latin, means "spirit present"—the ancients saw inspiration, perspicacity, and insight as gifts bestowed by ethereal powers, sometimes called daemons, a term that only much later took on negative connotations.

In that vein, I particularly like Murphy's observation: "If there's any fear or worry or anxiety in your thinking, you are not thinking at all. It's the mass mind or the law of averages thinking in you...." The hive mentality is my definition of negative thinking. It is conformist, often cynical, and passive: the opposite of all that is positive thinking in the sense that I use the term. I am sure that Murphy, however different our cultural reference points, would have agreed.

"Ideas are your masters," Murphy writes. Is that true? Certainly ideas of self-image, barring some over-whelming countervailing force, shape your existence. By contrast, ersatz and repetitive ideas come from mass viewpoints, conditioning, and self-imposed limits. Authentic ideas come from your unconditioned self. Allow this collection to help you enter the full possibility of that truth and its meaning.

—*Mitch Horowitz*

The Master Key to Wealth

The whole world and all its treasures, the sea, air, and earth were here when you were born. Begin to think of the untold and undiscovered riches all around you, waiting for the intelligence of man to bring them forth. Look at wealth as the air you breathe. Get that attitude of mind.

As Emerson said to the woman who wanted to prosper, he took her down to the ocean and said, "Take a look."

She said, "Oh, there's plenty of water, isn't there?"

He said, "Look at wealth that way, and you'll always have it." Realize it's like the tide forever flowing out, forever flowing back.

A sales manager said to me that an associate of his sold a million-dollar idea for expansion to the organization. You can have an idea worth a fortune, too. Wealth is a thought image in your mind. Wealth is an idea in your mind. Wealth is a mental attitude. He also told me that there were more millionaires now in the United States than at any time in the history of the country.

You can have an idea worth a fortune. Moreover, you are here to release the imprisoned splendor within you and surround yourself with luxury, beauty, and the riches of life. Learn that it is necessary to have the right attitude toward money, wealth, food, raiment, clothing, all these things. When you really make friends with wealth, you will always have a surplus of it.

It is normal and natural for you to desire a fuller, richer, happier, and more wonderful life. Look upon money as God's idea of maintaining the economic health of the nation, of the nations of the world. When money is circulating freely in your life, you're economically healthy. In the same manner as when your blood is circulating freely, you're free from congestion.

Begin now to see money in its true significance and role in life as a symbol of exchange. That's all it is. It has taken many forms down through the ages. Money, to you, should mean freedom from want. It should mean beauty, luxury, abundance, sense of security, and refinement. You're entitled to it.

Being poor is a disease. It is a mental attitude. A young woman, a very good writer who had been accepted for publication said to me one time, "I don't write for money."

I said to her, "What's wrong with money? It's true you don't write for money, but the laborer is worthy of his hire. What you write inspires, lifts up, and encourages others. When you adopt the right attitude, financial compensation will automatically come to you freely and copiously."

She actually disliked money. Once she referred to money as "filthy lucre." Going back, I suppose, to the early days where she heard Mother or somebody say money is evil, or the love of money is the root of all evil, and all these things without any understanding at all. It's a rank superstition to say money is evil or a filthy lucre.

This woman had a subconscious pattern that there was some virtue in poverty. There isn't. It's a sickness, a disease. I explained to her that there was no evil in the universe and that good and evil were in the thoughts and motivations of man. All evil comes from misinterpretations of life and misuses of the laws of mind. In other words, the only evil is ignorance, and the only consequence is suffering.

It would be foolish to pronounce uranium, silver, lead, copper, iron, cobalt, nickel, calcium, or a dollar bill evil. How absurd, grotesque, and stupid that is. The only difference between one metal and another is the number and rate of motions of electrons revolving around a central nucleus.

A piece of paper such as a $100 bill is innocuous, and the only difference between it and copper or lead is that the atoms and molecules with their electrons and protons are arranged differently. Here is a simple technique she practiced which multiples wealth in her experience:

"My writings go forth to bless, heal, inspire, elevate, and dignify the minds and hearts of men and women, and I am divinely compensated in a wonderful way. I look upon money as divine substance, for everything is made from the one spirit. I know matter and spirit are one. Money is constantly circulating in my life, and I use it wisely and constructively. Money flows to me freely, joyously, and endlessly. Money is an idea in the mind of God. It is good and very good."

That's a wonderful prayer. It eradicates that superstitious nonsense about money being evil and things of that nature, or that there's some virtue in poverty, or the Lord loves the poor. All of that is rank superstition. It is frightful ignorance. That's all it is.

This young lady's changed attitude toward money has worked wonders in her life. It will work wonders in your life, too. She has completely eradicated that strange, superstitious belief that money was filthy lucre. She realized that her silent condemnation of money caused money to fly from her instead of to her. Her income has tripled in three months which was just the beginning of her financial prosperity.

*   *   *

Some years ago, I talked with a clergyman who had a very good following. He had an excellent knowledge of the laws of mind and was able to impart this knowledge to others, but he could never make ends meet. He had what he thought was a good alibi for his plight by quoting from Timothy. *"For the love of money is the root of all evil."*

That's in the Book of Timothy in the sixth chapter, 10th verse, forgetting what followed in the 17th verse of the same chapter. In other words, taking it out of context. When Paul charges the people to place their trust or faith in the living God, *"Who giveth us richly all things to enjoy?"* That's also in the Book of Timothy.

Love in Biblical language is to give your allegiance, loyalty, and faith to the source of all things, which is God or the living spirit or the life principle in you. You are not, therefore, to give your allegiance, loyalty, and trust to created things, but to the Creator, to the eternal source of everything in the universe, the source of your own breath, the source of your life, the source of the hair on your head, the source of your heartbeat, the source of the sun and the moon and the stars, the source of the world and the earth you walk on.

A man says, "All I want is money, and nothing else. That's my God, and nothing but money matters." He can get it, of course, but he's here to lead a balanced life. Man must also claim peace, harmony, beauty, guidance, love, joy, and wholeness in all phases of his life. How can he live without courage, faith, love, goodwill, and joy in this world today?

There's nothing wrong with money, not a thing in the world, but that's not the sole aim in life. To make money the sole aim in life would constitute an error, a wrong choice. There wouldn't be anything evil in it, but you'd be imbalanced or lopsided.

You must express your hidden talents. You must find your true place in life. You must experience a joy of contributing to the growth, happiness, and success of others. We're all here to give and give of your talents to the world. God gave you everything. God gave you Himself.

You have a tremendous debt to pay because you owe everything you have to the infinite, therefore you're here to give life and love and truth to your ideals, to your dreams, your aspirations. You're here to row the boat and put your hand to the wheel, contribute to the success and happiness, not only of your children but of the whole world.

To accumulate money to the exclusion of everything else causes a man to become imbalanced, lopsided and frustrated. Yes, as you apply the laws of your subconscious in the right way, you can have all the money you want and still have peace of mind, harmony, wholeness, and serenity.

You can do a lot of good with it. You can use it wisely, judiciously, and constructively, like anything in nature. You can use your knowledge of philosophy in a constructive way, or you can begin to brainwash impressionable minds with Communism and all the rest of it.

I pointed out to this minister how he was completely misinterpreting the scripture in pronouncing pieces of paper and metal as evil when these were neutral substances, for there is nothing good or bad, but thinking makes it so. He began to see all the good he could do with more money for his wife, family, and parishioners. He changed his attitude and let go of his superstition.

He began to claim boldly, regularly, and systemically:

"Infinite Spirit reveals better ways for me to serve. I am inspired and illumined from on high, and I give a divine transfusion of faith and confidence in the one presence and power to all those who hear me. I look upon money as God's idea, and it is constantly circulating in my life and that of all the people who surround me. We use it wisely, judiciously, and constructively under God's guidance and God's wisdom."

This young clergyman made a habit of this prayer, knowing that it would activate the powers of his subconscious mind. Today he has a beautiful church, which he wanted. The people built it for him. He has a radio program and has all the money he needs for his personal, worldly, and cultural needs. I can assure you, he no longer criticizes money. If you do, it will fly away from you because you're condemning that which you're praying for.

Now, follow this technique which I'm going to outline for you, and you'll never want for wealth all the days of your life, for it is the master key to wealth.

The first step is to reason it out in your mind that God or the life principle or the living spirit is the source of the universe, the galaxies in space, and everything you see, whether you look at the stars in the sky, the mountains, the lakes, the deposits in the earth and the sea, or all animals and plants. The life principle gave birth to you, and all the powers, qualities, and attributes of God are within you.

Come to a simple conclusion that everything you see and are aware of came out of the invisible mind of the infinite or the life principle, and that everything that man has invented, created, or made came out of the invisible mind of man, and the mind of man and the mind of God are one, for there's only one mind. That mind is common to all individual men. Everyone is an inlet and outlet to all that is.

Come now to a clear-cut decision that God is the source of your supply of energy, vitality, health, creative ideas, the source of the sun, the air you breathe, the apple you eat, and the money in your pocket, for everything is made inside and out of the invisible. It is as easy for God to become wealth in your life as it is to become a blade of grass or a crystal of snow.

The second step is to decide now to engrave in your subconscious mind the idea of wealth. Ideas are conveyed to the subconscious by repetition, faith, and expectancy. By repeating a thought pattern or an act over and over again, it becomes automatic, and your subconscious being compulsive, you will be compelled to express it. The pattern is the same as learning to walk, swim, play the piano, type, or drive a car.

You must believe in what you are affirming. It's not mumbo jumbo. It's not idle affirmations. You must believe in what you're affirming like when you put seeds in the ground and they grow after their kind. The seeds are thoughts deposited in your own subconscious mind.

You can imagine the seeds going from your conscious to your subconscious mind and being reproduced on the screen of space. By watering and fertilizing these seeds, you accelerate their growth.

Know what you are doing and why you are doing it. You're writing it with your conscious pen and your subconscious mind because you know wealth is a walk down the street and you see it. Can you count the flowers along the road as you drive? Can you count the sands in the seashore? Can you count the stars in the sky? Can you count the wealth that you're walking on, underneath you, maybe oil, gold, silver, uranium? Did you ever think of the riches of the sea, the soil, the air?

The third step is to repeat the following affirmation for about five minutes night and morning:

"I am now writing in my subconscious mind the idea of God's wealth. God is the source of my supply, and I know God is the life principle within me, and I know I am alive, and all my needs are met at every moment of time and point of space. God's wealth flows freely, joyously, and ceaselessly into my experience, and I give thanks for God's riches forever circulating in my experience."

Step four, when thoughts of lack come to you such as, "I can't afford that trip," or, "I can't meet that note in the bank," or, "I can't pay that bill," never, ever finish a negative statement about finances. This is mandatory. Reverse it immediately in your mind by affirming, "God is my instant and everlasting supply, and that bill is paid in divine order."

If a negative thought comes to you 50 times in one hour, reverse it each time by thinking and affirming, "God is my instant supply meeting that need right now." After a while, the thought of financial lack will lose all momentum, and you will find your subconscious is being conditioned to wealth.

If you look at a new car, for example, never say, "I can't buy that," or, "I can't afford it." Your subconscious takes you literally and blocks all your good. On the contrary, say to yourself, "That car is for sale. It is a divine idea, and I accept it in divine order, through divine love."

This is the master key to wealth. It's impossible for any sincere person to practice this technique and not have all the wealth he or she needs, all the days of their life.

Follow it, and you're setting the law of opulence in operation. It will work for you as well as for anybody else. The law of mind is no respecter of persons. Your thoughts make you wealthy or poor. Choose the riches of life right here and right now.

• • •

A sales manager sent me one of his men for counseling. This salesman was a brilliant college graduate. He knew his products very well. He was in a lucrative territory but was making only $5,000 annually in commissions. The sales manager felt he should double or at least triple it.

In talking to the young man, I found he was down on himself. He had developed a subconscious pattern or self-image of $5,000 a year. In other words, that's all I'm worth. He said that he had been born in a poverty-stricken home and that his parents had told him that he was destined to be poor. His stepfather had always told him, "You'll never amount to anything. You're dumb, you're stupid." These thoughts were accepted by his impressionable mind, and he was experiencing his subconscious belief in lack and limitation.

I explained to him that he could change his subconscious mind by feeding it with life-giving patterns. Accordingly, I gave him a metal and spiritual formula to follow which would transform his life. I explained to him that he should, under no circumstances, deny what he affirmed. Your subconscious mind accepts your convictions, what you really believe. So, believe in God's wealth and God's riches, which are all around you.

He affirmed every morning before going to work:

"I am born to succeed. I am born to win. The infinite within me can't fail. Divine law and order govern my life. Divine peace fills my soul. Divine love saturates my mind. Infinite intelligence guides me in all ways. God's riches flow to me freely, joyously, endlessly, ceaselessly. I'm advancing, moving forward, and growing mentally, spiritually, financially, and in all other ways. I know these truths are sinking into my subconscious mind, and I believe they will grow after their kind."

A year later when I met this young man again, I discovered that he had been transformed. He had absorbed these ideas which we had discussed, and he said, "I am appreciating life now, and wonderful things have happened. I have an income of $25,000 this year, five times greater than the previous year." He has learned the simple truth that whatever he inscribes in his subconscious mind becomes effective and functional in his life. That power is within you. You can use it as well.

The young boy who is operating the machine while I'm broadcasting is named Robbie Wright. He told me about his uncle who used to work in a bank, and this uncle wanted to make more money for his wife and his children. He was always affirming, "God is my instant supply and divinely guided, and always infinite, spirit opens up a new door."

Well, he told me that his uncle was in town about two months ago and that his salary is now $200,000 a year, all his expenses paid, yet he was only getting $40,000 when he started to realize the truth about himself. He's able to do great things and live a wonderful life.

All this is an idea, an idea in his mind. Wealth is an idea. A radio is an idea. Television is an idea. An automobile is an idea. Everything you look at is an idea.

Supposing you destroyed all the automobiles in the world due to some holocaust. Well, an engineer could run them off, couldn't he? We'd have millions of them in no time. Use the following meditation for assurance in achieving find wealth:

"'Thou madest him to have dominion over the works of thy hands.' I know that my faith in God determines my future. My faith in God means my faith in all things good. I unite myself now with true ideas, and I know that future will be the image and likeness of my habitual thinking. As a man thinketh in his heart or subconscious, so is he.

"From this moment forward, my thoughts are on. 'Whatsoever things are true, whatsoever things

convince your deeper mind that you have the thing you want, it will immediately bring it to pass.

You might say to me, "How can I convince my deeper mind, my subconscious, that I have riches or any other good thing when my common sense tells me that bills are piling up, creditors are after me, the bank is calling up to pay for the mortgage for the money I owe, and so on?" You can't if you keep thinking about debts and obligations and how much you owe. You'll only magnify your misery.

Here is a truth about the laws of your mind: Your deeper mind accepts as a fact whatever you repeat to it in convincing tones, often enough, just the same as you learned to walk. Your thought pattern, an act, whether it's swimming or walking or playing tennis or golf, and you repeat it over and over again. You knew what you were doing and why you were doing it. You wanted to learn to walk, you wanted to learn to dance, you wanted to learn to swim.

Finally your subconscious assimilated the pattern, and then you swam automatically, and you walked automatically. It's the same procedure in praying for wealth or anything else. Once your subconscious accepts the statement as a fact, it proceeds to do everything possible to bring riches to you.

That's the whole purpose of affirmations, so that you convince yourself of the truth of that which you affirm. Then, your deeper mind will bring these things to pass.

Many men say to me, "Oh, I got an affirmation from someone, and it said I am rich and prosperous now. I'm successful, and I'm very wealthy. But that affirmation succeeded in making me much more aware of my need." Because he believed more in poverty and lack than he did in the riches all around him.

So I explained to him, "You must turn away from that pattern and come back. Change your belief. Your subconscious accepts what you believe.

"Look around you. Realize that God created you and the whole world. It's an invisible spirit within you. Everything is made inside and out of it. It started your heartbeat. It's the air you breathe, the water you drink, it's the fruit that you eat.

"Therefore, turn away, and turn within, and change that and say, 'I recognize the eternal source of my supply. God is the source of my supply. All my needs, spiritual, mental, material, are met at every moment of time and point of space, and God's wealth is circulating in my life, and there's always a surplus, so that by night I'm advancing, moving forward and growing spiritually, mentally, materially, financially, intellectually, and every way.

"'All things be ready if the mind be so. It is done unto me as I believe and, before they call I will answer.

While they're yet speaking, I will hear. Oh, how I love the law. Let it be my meditation both day and night, and the law is, I am, what I contemplate. I am what I believe myself to be. According to my faith is it done unto me.' God gave you richly all things to enjoy. God made you rich. Why then are you poor?"

As he began to realize the source of the infinite ocean of supply, the source of the very hair on his head, the source of the power that enables him to lift a chair, the source of the grass, the source of the hay in the field, the source of the cattle in a thousand hills, he began to realize the source. He aligned himself with it, and then it made sense to him. Then he realized that he was writing in his subconscious mind the idea of wealth, of growth, and prosperity.

He changed his belief to a belief in the endless riches all around him instead of poverty, which was a false belief in his mind. Don't you know enough fruit rots in the tropics to feed all humanity? Nature is lavish, extravagant, bountiful. God gave you richly all things to enjoy.

"*These things,*" he said, "*I've said unto you that my joy might remain in you, and your joy might be full. Heretofore, you've asked for nothing; now ask that your joy might be full. I am come that you might have life and have it more abundantly. Heretofore, you've asked for nothing; now ask that your joy might full."* But to ask, you see, in the Bible is to claim.

As Paul says, *"You claim it boldly,"* but you know what you're doing and why you're doing it. So, if you have a lot of debts and obligations, a lot of bills to pay, don't worry about them. Turn to the source, which is endless. Remember the farmer, what he says to you. He says, "I don't worry about the weeds. The grain is growing, and it will kill all the weeds." That's what the farmer tells you.

Likewise, as you focus on your good, on guidance and right action and the eternal source of your supply, whether it is mental or spiritual or financial you need, there is but one source, not two. As you turn to it and give thanks for that endless supply, then all the weeds will be killed. Thoughts of lack and limitation will die in you, and God will multiply your good exceedingly.

Bring joy into your life. Pray for joy by claiming it. *"The joy of the Lord is my strength,"* the Bible says. Repeat that to yourself, and after a while, you'll be amazed what will happen to your bloodstream and to the general circulation. Don't keep analyzing it or gritting your teeth about it. Just know that joy is the expression of life.

Don't run like a horse at it. Use no willpower, no muscle power. No blood vessel power is involved in this mental and spiritual therapeutic technique. Just know and claim that the joy of the Lord is flowing through you now, and wonders will happen as you pray this way. Freedom and peace of mind will be yours as a result. If you have peace of mind, you'll have peace in your pocketbook and in your home and in your relationship with people, for peace is the power at the heart of God.

•   •   •

"There is a river, the streams whereof make glad the city of my God." The city of God is your mind. The people who dwell there, well you know very well who dwells there: your thoughts, ideas, images, beliefs, opinions. Make sure they conform to the divine standard.

A woman said to me, "I was blocked financially. I had reached the point where I had not enough money for food for the children. All I had was $5. I held it in my hand and said, 'God will multiply this exceedingly according to His riches and glory. I am now filled with the riches of the infinite. All my needs are instantaneously met now and all the days of my life.'"

She believed that. They weren't idle words. You don't gain the ear of God by vain repetitions. You must know what you're doing and why you're doing it. You must know that your conscious mind is a pen, and you're writing something, engraving something in your subconscious mind.

Whatever you impress your subconscious mind with will be expressed on the screen of space. It'll come forth as form, function, experience, and events, good or bad, so make sure you plant that which is lovely and of good report.

She said, "I affirmed that all my needs are instantaneously met now and all the days of my life for about half an hour, and a great sense of peace came over me. I spent the $5 freely for food. The owner of the market asked me if I wanted to work there as a cashier, since the present one had just gotten married and left. I accepted it, and shortly afterward, I married the owner, my boss, and we have experienced and are experiencing all the riches of life."

This woman looked to the source. She didn't know how her prayer would be answered because you never know the workings of the subconscious. She believed in her heart, and the blessings of the infinite followed. To believe is to live in the state of being it. It also means to be alive to the eternal truths. Her good was magnified and multiplied exceedingly because the subconscious always magnifies what you give attention to.

There is a presence and a power within you, and you can use it. You can stir up, as Paul says, "The gift of God within you," for God is the giver of the gift, and everything has been given to you, and therefore you can tune in and claim guidance, right action, beauty, love, peace, abundance, security. You can say to yourself, "God's ideas unfold within me, bringing me harmony, health, peace, and joy."

If you're in business, you're a professional man, you're an artist, you're an inventor, just sit down quietly, and say, "God reveals to me new, creative ideas, original, wonderful ideas which bless humanity in countless ways." Then, watch the wonderful ideas come to you, and they will come because when you call, it answers.

Remember what it says in the Bible: "*Call upon me, I'll answer you. I'll be with you in trouble. I set you on high because you hath known my name.*" The name means the nature. The nature of infinite intelligence is responsiveness. Call, and the response comes.

Constantly affirm, feel, and believe that God multiplies your good exceedingly, and you will be enriched every moment of the day spiritually, mentally, intellectually, financially, and socially, for there's no end to the glory of man for his daily living.

Watch the wonders that will happen as you impress these truths in your subconscious mind. Let these truths sink into your subconscious, and they will, and they are. You're engraving them, and the more often you do this, well the quicker you will impregnate your deeper mind. You'll experience a glorious future in a financial way—in every way.

Watch your thoughts. Never talk about economic lack and limitation. Never talk about being poor or in want. It is very foolish to talk to your neighbors or relatives about hard times, financial problems, and like matters.

Count your blessings. Begin to think prosperous thoughts. Talk about the divine riches present everywhere. Realize that the feeling of wealth produces wealth.

When you talk about not having enough to go around and how little you have and how you must cut corners and eat the cheapest meat, these thoughts are created, and you are only impoverishing yourself. Use the money freely. Release it with joy, and realize that God's wealth flows to you in avalanches of abundance.

Look up to the source. As you turn to the divine presence within you, the response will come. It is written, *"He careth for you."* You will find neighbors, strangers, associates adding to your good and also to your supply of material things. Make it a practice to pray for divine guidance in all your ways, and believe that God or the supreme intelligence is supplying all your needs according to His riches in glory.

Claim it boldly. *"Come boldly to the throne of grace,"* Paul says, and grace when it's removed from its mystique is simply the mathematical, orderly reflection of your habitual thinking and imagery. In other words, there's supreme intelligence that responds to your conscious thinking and imagery.

Pray for divine guidance, in all your ways. As you make a habit of this attitude of mind, you will find the invisible law of opulence can and will produce visible riches for you.

• • •

Recently a doctor told me that her constant prayer was as follows. "I live in the joyous expectancy of the best, and invariably the best comes to me."

"My favorite Bible verse," she said, "with which I saturate my mind is, 'He giveth to all life and breath and all things.'" That's from the Book of Acts, 17th chapter, 25th verse.

She has learned that she is not dependent on people for joy, health, success, and happiness or peace of mind. She looks to the living spirit Almighty within her for promotion, achievement, wealth, success, and happiness. *"Whosoever trusteth in the Lord, happy is he."* That's from the Book of Proverbs, 16th chapter, 20th verse.

Contemplate promotion, success, achievement, illumination, and inspiration, and the spirit of the Almighty will move on your behalf, compelling you to express fully what you meditate on. Let go now, and permit the infinite riches of the infinite one to open up new doors for you. Let wonders happen in your life.

In prayer therapy, avoid struggle and strain. Don't try to force things. How could you add power to omnipotence? Can you make a seed grow? You can't. Plant it in the ground. It will grow. The oak is in the acorn. The apple is in the apple seed. The archetype or pattern is there, but you must deposit it in the soil where it dies, undergoes dissolution, bequeaths its energy to another form of itself. A spiritual-minded man looks at an acorn and sees a forest.

That's the way your subconscious works. It magnifies your good exceedingly. So avoid strain, since this attitude is indicative of your unbelief. If you're worried and fearful and anxious, that inhibits your good. That brings about blocks and delays and impediments in your life.

What does fear do? *"That which I greatly feared has come upon me."* Reverse it. That which I greatly love comes into my experience. Love is emotional attachment.

All the wisdom and power necessary to solve any problem is in your subconscious. Your conscious mind is prone to look at external conditions and tends to struggle and resist. Remember it is the quiet mind that gets things done.

Quiet your body periodically. Tell it to be still and relaxed. It has to obey you. Your body moves as moved upon. Your body acts as acted upon. Your body has no self-conscious intelligence, no volition, no will. It moves as moved upon. You can play a melody of God in your body.

When your conscious mind is quiet and receptive, the wisdom of your subconscious rises to the surface mind, and you receive your solution.

A beauty parlor operator told me that the secret of her success was that every morning prior to opening her beauty salon, she had a quiet period in which she affirmed:

"God's peace fills my soul, and God's love saturates my whole being. God guides, prospers, and inspires me. I am illumined from on high, and His healing love flows from me to all my clients.

"Divine love comes in my door; divine love goes out of my door. All those who come into my salon are blessed, healed, and inspired. The infinite healing presence saturates the whole place. 'This is the day the Lord hath made, and I rejoice and give thanks,' for the countless blessings which come to my clients and to myself."

She had this prayer written out on a card and reiterated these truths every morning. At night, she gave thanks for all her clients, claiming that they were guided, prospered, happy, and harmonious, and that

God and His love flowed through each one, filling up all the empty vessels in her life.

She stated to me that by following this prayer technique pattern, at the end of three months she had far more clients than she could handle and had to hire three additional operators. She had discovered the riches of effective prayer and is prospering beyond her fondest dreams.

A sales manager told me that he had been fired because of excessive drinking on the job and because of being involved with one of the secretaries in the office. He was very distressed, dejected, worried about his wife, his income, and his future.

In talking with his wife later, I discovered that she was a chronic nagger and had tried unsuccessfully to dominate and control her husband. She was abnormally jealous and very possessive, and she clocked him in every evening creating a scene if he were not home at a certain hour.

He was emotionally and spiritually immature and did not handle the matter at all constructively. He deeply resented her nagging and her clocking of his arrival at home and retaliated by drinking and becoming involved with another woman. He said to me, "I just wanted to get even with her."

Both of them agreed it takes two to make a good marriage. It takes two to prosper. If a husband and wife will agree in prosperity and success—agreement means harmony—they will prosper. They'll have all the money they need to do what they want to do when they want to do it, and when you have all the wealth you need to do what you want to do, when you want to do it, you're as rich as Croesus.

Both of them agreed to start a prayer process night and morning, realizing that as they prayed for each other, there could not possibly be any bitterness, hostility, or resentment, as divine love casts out everything unlike itself.

She prayed night and morning as follows:

"My husband is God's man. God is guiding him to his true place. What he is seeking is seeking him. Divine love fills his soul. Divine peace fills his mind and heart. He is prospered in all his ways spiritually, mentally, financially, socially every way. By day and by night, he's advancing, moving forward, and growing spiritually, mentally, financially, socially, intellectually, in all ways, for life itself is growth. There is harmony, peace, love, and understanding between us. It is divine right action and divine peace operating in our lives."

He prayed for his wife night and morning as follows:

"My wife is God's child. She's a daughter of the infinite, a child of eternity. Divine love fills her soul, and it is written He careth for her. Divine love, peace, harmony, and joy flow through her at all times. She's divinely guided and prospered in all her ways, for to prosper is to grow along all lines. There is harmony, peace, love, and understanding between us. I salute the divinity in her, and she salutes the divinity in me."

As both of them became relaxed and peaceful about the situation, they realized that only good can come out of this. Soon he received a phone call from the president of the company calling him back, stating that he had heard he'd had a reconciliation with his wife and at the same time praised him for his past achievements and accomplishments for the organization.

Actually, his wife, without his knowledge, had visited the president of the company and had told him the whole story, how happy they now were and how the other woman had vanished out of his life. She told how they were now praying together. He was impressed, and she and her husband discovered very quickly the riches of scientific prayer, for the riches of the infinite are within you.

•　•　•

You can know if you have succeeded in prayer by the way you feel. If you remain worried or anxious, or if you're wondering how, when, and where or through what source your answer will come, you are meddling. This indicates you do not really trust the wisdom of your subconscious. Avoid nagging yourself all day long or even from time to time.

When you think of your desire, lightness of touch is important. Remind yourself that infinite intelligence is taking care of it in divine order, far better than you can by tenseness of your conscious mind. For example, if you say, "Well, I need $5,000 by the fifteenth of next month," or "The judge must make a decision for me by the first of the month, otherwise I lose my home, my mortgage, and so on," that's fear and anxiety and tension. What will that do? Bring blocks, delays, impediments, and difficulties into your life.

Always go to the source. Remember, "in peace and confidence shall be your strength." When you're anxious and tense and worried, that will not bring about prosperity, peace of mind, health, or anything else. Go back to the source.

Come to a place of absolute rest in your mind and say to yourself, reiterate these truths:

"It is done unto me as I believe. Go thy way as thou has believed, so be it done unto thee. All things be ready if

the mind be so," which means all I have to do is ready my mind to receive the benediction, the guidance, the wealth, the answer, the solution, the way out.

"According to my faith is it done unto me."

"Go thy way. Thy faith hath made thee whole. Go in peace; thy faith hath made thee whole."

"All things are ready if the mind be so."

"The light of God shines in me. The peace of the everlasting God fills my soul."

"In quietness and confidence shall be my strength."

"God gave me richly all things to enjoy."

"With God all things are possible."

Reiterate these simple truths, and say, *"'The Lord is my shepherd, I shall not want. He maketh me lie down in green pastures. He leadeth me beside the still waters. He restoreth my soul.' When I call upon Him and He answers me, He'll be with me in trouble. He'll set me on high because he hath known my name. God is my instant and everlasting supply, an ever-present help in times of trouble."*

Read a Psalm like the 23rd and 91st Psalms, and go over these Psalms quietly, peacefully, and lovingly. You'll get to a point of rest and peace in your mind, and you'll realize that God is never late, and that God is your instant and everlasting supply guiding and directing you, revealing to you everything you need

abundance, security, and goodwill in the garden of my mind. The mind is God's garden.

"The glory and beauty of God will be expressed in my life, and I will know my garden will yield an abundant harvest. From this moment forward, I express life, love, and truth. I am radiantly happy and prosperous in all my ways, and God multiplies my good exceedingly."

To prosper means to succeed, to thrive, to turn out well. In other words, when you are prospering, you're expanding, growing spiritually, mentally, financially, socially, and intellectually.

Never be envious or jealous of another person's wealth or promotion, or their diamonds or jewels, for that would impoverish you. That would attract lack and limitation to you. Rejoice in their success, their prosperity, and their wealth and wish for them greater riches because what you wish for the other, you're wishing for yourself, for you're the only thinker. What you think about the other, you're creating in your own mind, body, and experience and also your pocketbook. This is why you rejoice in the success and the prosperity in the millions that others have.

In order to truly prosper, it is necessary that you become a channel through which the life principle flows freely, harmoniously, joyously, and lovingly. I suggest that you establish a definite method of working and thinking, that you practice it regularly and systematically every day.

. . .

One young man who consulted me had experienced a poverty complex for many years and had received no answers to his prayer. He had prayed for prosperity, but the fear of poverty continuously weighed on his mind. Naturally, he attracted more lack and limitation than prosperity.

The subconscious mind accepts the dominant of two ideas. Change your mind from belief in poverty, but begin to believe in God's riches which are all around you, infinite riches.

After talking with me, he began to realize that his thought image of wealth produces wealth, that every thought is creative unless it is neutralized by a counter thought of greater intensity. Furthermore, he realized that his thought and belief about poverty was greater than his belief in the infinite riches all around him.

Consequently, he changed his thoughts and kept them changed. I wrote out a prosperity prayer for him as follows. It will benefit you.

"I know there is only one source, the life principle, the living spirit from which all things flow. It created the universe and all things therein contained. I'm a focal point of the divine presence. My mind is open and receptive. I am a free-flowing channel for harmony, beauty, guidance, wealth, and the riches of the infinite.

"I know that wealth, health, and success are released from within and appear on the without. I am now in harmony with the infinite riches within and without, and I know these thoughts are sinking into my subconscious mind and will be reflected on the screen of space. I wish for everyone all the blessings of life. I am open and receptive to the divine riches, spiritual, mental, and material. They flow to me in avalanches of abundance."

This young man focused his thoughts on God's riches rather than on poverty and made it a special point never to deny what he affirmed. Many people pray for wealth, and they deny it an hour later. They say, "I can't afford this. I can't make ends meet." They're making a mockery of their prayer.

They're like the man who gets into a taxi in New York, and he's going to the airport, and on the way he says to the taxi driver, "Take me back home. I forgot my passport." So, he goes back. Then, he says, "Oh, I better go to my club. I forgot my wallet." So, the taxi driver takes him to his club, and he says, "Oh, I forgot some letters at my grandmother's," so off he goes to the grandmother.

He gives half a dozen directions in half an hour to the taxi driver. Finally, the taxi driver takes him to the police station because he realizes he's mental.

This is the way millions of people pray, even in the New Thought movement. They give half a dozen directions to their subconscious mind within half an hour. The subconscious is so confused and perplexed, it doesn't know what to do. It doesn't do anything, so it results in frustration.

You don't put a seed in the ground and then dig it up. Stop contradicting what you affirmed. That's the way people pray for prosperity, constantly denying what they're affirming, and they're making a mockery of prayer.

So this young man focused his thoughts on God's riches rather than poverty, and he stopped saying, "I can't buy that piano, or I can't buy that car." Never use the word "can't." Can't is the only devil in the universe. Your subconscious takes you literally and blocks all your good.

In a month's time, his whole life was transformed. He affirmed the above truths, which I just mentioned, morning and evening for about ten minutes, slowly and quietly, engraving them in his mind, knowing what he was doing, believing what he was doing, knowing that he was actually writing down these truths in his sub-conscious mind causing the latter to be activated and to release its hidden treasures. For the gold mine is in your subconscious. The diamond mine is there, it's the source of all the riches of Heaven.

Although this man had been a salesman for ten years with rather dim prospects for the future, suddenly he was made sales manager at $30,000 a year plus prime benefits. Your subconscious has ways that you know not of.

It's impossible to impregnate your subconscious mind with the idea of wealth and be poor. It's impossible to impregnate your subconscious with the idea of success, and you were born to win, to succeed. The infinite can't fail. You're born to triumph.

"Son, thou art ever with me, and all that I hath is thine." Let your prayer be,

"By day and by night I'm advancing, moving forward, and growing. God gave me richly all things to enjoy."

The Fourth Way
to Pray

The Book of Daniel says, "*These three men, Shadrach, Meshach, and Abednego, fell down bound in the midst of the burning, fiery furnace. Then, Nebuchadnezzar, the king, was astonished and rose up in haste and spake, and said unto his counselors, 'Did we not cast three men bound into the midst of the fire?' They answered and said unto the king, 'True, O King.' He answered and said, 'Lo, I see four men loose, walking in the midst of the fire, and they have no hurt. The form of the fourth is like under the Son of God.'*" That's from the third chapter of Daniel.

The fourth man in the fiery furnace is the consciousness of God, the awareness of the living sprit Almighty within you. It means you're an exalted state of mind; you're in tune with the infinite. The ancient scripture says water wets it not, fire burns it not, wind blows it not away, and swords pierce it not. When man is in a certain state of mind, a higher spiritual dimension, fire does not burn him, and poisons do not kill.

F. L. Rawson, the great English electrical scientist, wrote about the experience of one of his associates, who in a clairvoyant vision saw an airplane come out of the clouds in flames. It burned out about one hundred feet from the ground, then cracked and fell. She knew this was going to happen, knew the place and the time. She looked about to see what the men were like, and she couldn't distinguish anything about them. They were burnt to a cinder.

She went to the house of a friend which overlooked a field and at half past 2 p.m. asked the lady of the house to come up and help her. The two stood there praying. Suddenly, the airplane, which she'd seen in a clairvoyant vision, came out aflame. It burned and cracked just as she had seen in her vision. There were two men in it, and they were absolutely untouched. It was like the case of Shadrach, Meshach, and Abednego. They were not even singed.

One of them said, "I was about to throw myself out when suddenly a sense of absolute peace and safety came, and I sat back in the machine." There he was in a furnace. That man turned out to be the son of the lady she had asked to come up and help her.

There are many such cases recorded all over the world. The three men mentioned in Daniel represent faith, love, and understanding. "Faith," of course, means your definite belief that there is a response from infinite intelligence when you call upon it.

"Love" in the Bible means allegiance, loyalty, and devotion to the one power, for there is only one power.

I am, and there is none else, recognizing no other cause and positively refusing to give power to any person, place, or thing, any created thing in the universe. In other words, you put the Creator first in your life. That's called love in the Bible.

"Understanding" means you stand on your confidence, trust, and insight into the working of the law, knowing whatever you believe in your heart will come to fruition.

The fourth way to pray is to contemplate the presence of God, the infinite within you. There cannot be two infinites. Infinity cannot be divided or multiplied.

The two women mentioned by Rawson prayed by practicing the presence of God where the plane was. In other words, they contemplated the presence of love, peace, harmony, beauty, and divine right action, and in their minds and hearts immersed these men in the holy omnipresence aided by the light of God, and they succeeded in saving their lives. Had they had 100% realization, which means to make it real, they could have saved the plane as well.

•   •   •

Joseph Chilton Pearce, a research scholar, states that in Surrey, England, in 1935 and 1936, the English Society for Psychical Research ran a series of tests on two Indian fakirs imported expressly for the purpose. The tests were graded by physicians, chemists, physicists, and psychologists of Oxford and Cambridge. The Indians walked the fire under controlled conditions, under the skeptical and probing eyes of science itself.

No chemicals were used, no preparations made. They repeated the performances on demand under a variety of conditions, and over a period of several weeks. Surface temperatures were between 450 and 500 degrees centigrade, the interior temperature was 1,400 degrees centigrade. There was no trickery or hallucination.

Mr. Pearce pointed out that a high point was reached when one the fakirs noticed a professor of psychology avidly intrigued and dumbfounded. The fakir, sensing the longing, told the good professor he, too, could walk the fire if he so desired. By holding the fakir's hand, the good man was seized with faith that he could. He shed his shoes and hand in hand, they walked the fire ecstatic and unharmed.

You see, faith is an attitude of mind. It's a way of thinking. It's faith in the creative power, the one power that responds to you when you call upon it. All of us know fire burns, but when man tunes in with the infinite and reaches a high state of consciousness, he is immune. Neither does cancer have to kill a person if he decides to ascend in consciousness and definitely believes he will be healed.

omnipresent, an ever-present help in times of trouble, it responded to him.

The fourth way takes in all the knowledge of science, philosophy, and religion, plus an awareness, an exalted recognition of the presence of God in man. Science is constantly changing.

*   *   *

Some years ago, the late Robert Millikan of the California Institute of Technology pointed out that the dogma of immutable elements is gone. It went with the discovery of radioactivity. The two fundamental principles, conservation of mass and conservation of energy, are now gone as distinct, inseparable verities.

Today we're dealing with a universe of densities, frequencies, and intensities. It is a changing, evolving, dynamic, living universe. Everything in the universe is alive. Different degrees of aliveness or livingness, different degrees of intelligence. So the more intelligence that is resurrected in man, the greater measure of freedom does he have.

Einstein said that matter was energy reduced to the point of visibility. *Energy* is a term used by scientists for spirit, or God. Today, energy and mass are interconvertible and interchangeable.

Medicine is rapidly changing. A few weeks ago, I read an article by Dr. Rubenstein of UCLA. It was in

The Times, and he said that the medicine of ten years ago is completely outmoded due to a rapid advance in science and technology and that the doctor practicing according to standards of 1950 is completely out of date and may be dangerous. Chemistry and physics are also undergoing a rapid transformation, so much so that the textbooks of a few years ago are now out of date.

Religion is changing all over the world as well. *Dogmatism* means to assert something without knowledge, to assert something which every high school boy knows is false, such as the six days of creation and God rested on the seventh, and that Adam and Eve are the first parents in the Garden of Eden.

All that is utter nonsense. The Garden of Eden is our own subconscious mind, Adam and Eve is your conscious and subconscious mind. The harmonious interaction of your conscious and subconscious mind bring forth health, happiness, peace, abundance, and security.

Dogmatism is the attitude of a closed mind. It is foolish to talk about the six days of creation or the rotation of the sun about the earth. They believed the earth was flat at one time. Some people still do.

The Tree of Life is the living presence Almighty within you. The Tree of Good and Evil represents good and bad thoughts or ideas which, like a tree, become fixed and grow up into opinions, fixations, prejudices, and fears. The good ideas grow up too, such as the belief in the Golden Rule, of love and kindness and honesty and integrity. So, the good and evil are within ourselves, the Tree of Life and the Tree of Good and Evil are within all of us.

Voltaire said, "If God did not exist, it would be necessary to invent him." Science has made wonderful strides and has been a great boom and blessing to mankind.

In ancient times in Europe, when a plague hit a city, the priest would carry the host in a procession, pour holy water on the streets and people. I said to the audience on Sunday morning that holy water was water you boil Hell out of. So there isn't any such thing as holy water—water is just H_2O. It's the same water in Lourdes that's in your tap. There's no difference.

Science came along and introduced sanitation hygiene and saved countless lives. Lister, Pasteur, and other research men, through their discoveries, caused doctors to adopt sterilization procedures in hospitals thereby saving countless lives. Prior to that, people died like flies on the hospital table.

We have had wonderful philosophers, such as Plato, Aristotle, Socrates, Tagore, Emerson, William James, Kant, Plotinus, and Eckhart, and many others. They have set forth marvelous truths, but philosophy is not of much use except if we put it into practice.

Down through the ages, we've had frightful religious wars. Philosophers have argued among themselves, and science has not been able to solve the problems of the world. Each one is necessary and useful, but all three, science, philosophy, and religion, such as creed, dogma, and tradition, have failed miserably in bringing peace to the troubled mind.

We'll continue to have war as long as man is what he is, until man awakens to the presence and power of God within him and realizes the 3.5 billion people in this world are simply extensions of himself. There's only one mind, and then he realizes that whatever he wishes or thinks about another, he's creating in his own mind, body, pocketbook, and circumstances.

When he awakens to that simple truth, he will pour forth his benedictions on all mankind. He won't want to steal, rob, cheat, or defraud. There will be no avarice in his heart because he'll realize that whatever he can claim and feel to be true, the spirit will give to him.

Theologians talk about God instead of teaching men and women how to experience God in their hearts. There are many good, kind religious people. They follow all the tenets, rules, and regulations of their churches. They're conventionally good, but like Job, they suffer miserably. Hospitals and mental institutions are full of so-called good people who believe in personal saviors and so on.

You are your own savior. You answer your own prayer, because whatever you impress in your subconscious is expressed as form, function, experience, and events. A man who doesn't know this is living in the Dark Ages. He's a medievalist in his thinking, he's living in the jungle.

From an external standpoint, it is true that these so-called good people follow the liturgies and standards of their religious beliefs, but the law of mind is that as a man thinketh in his heart or subconscious, so is he, so does he act, so does he experience, so does he become.

It is the deep-seated belief in your subconscious that is made manifest. What you really believe in your heart is what you experience. If you work very hard, yet you believe in failure, you'll fail. You might be very good. You may be kind to the poor, visit hospitals, and tithe, and do all these things, but it's what you believe in your heart that is made manifest, not what you give theoretical assent to. It is not your nominal belief, but it is belief in the heart that matters. It is your emotional espousals that are made manifest.

For example, a person may go to church every day and receive sacraments, but fears the flu or some sickness, or fears failure. All these things will be experienced by him, for the law of the Lord is perfect, and

you can't think negatively and experience constructively and harmoniously.

Many people get a 100% in a philosophical exam-
ination, yet their lives are chaotic. They can quote
Plato and Aristotle and Emerson. They take Emerson in school as literature. If you followed the ideas
of Emerson, you'd be walking in the light. You'd be
walking along the shores of reality. You'd experience
the moment that lasts forever.

Emerson said, "Man is what he thinks all day long.
If your soul is erect, all goes well," meaning if you
exalt God in the midst of you. He called it "the great
over-soul within." These philosophical ideas are not
assimilated, appropriated, digested, or incorporated
in the subconscious mind. Head-knowledge is not
heart-knowledge. Science, philosophy, and religion
are necessary; each is doing good in its own way, but
don't forget to embrace them all under the banner of
the presence of God in you, the Almighty power.

An Air Force captain who was recently returned
from Vietnam told me that he parachuted out of his
plane in Vietnam and found himself in the jungle. He
had medical knowledge, being a doctor, and dressed
his own wounds. He had knowledge of science, and
he studied the philosophies of the world. He also
belonged to a nominal religious belief, but he said that

a few weeks previously, he had been reading some Unity literature sent to him by his sister from Los Angeles. He began to pray as follows:

> "I know God or Spirit is within me. It is all wise and is leading me to safety now. I knew that infinite intelligence would respond. I knew of its responsiveness and susceptibility because of reading New Thought literature.

A few minutes later, he said,

> "My brother appeared to me and said, 'I will order the medics to come for you. They will be here in half an hour.'"

In half an hour, the medics came on the scene and rescued him. He asked them, "How did you know I was here?" They explained that an officer appeared and gave them exact instructions.

He said, "Describe him," and the description fit his brother exactly, though his brother was killed in action a year previously. This is the fourth way. The answer comes in ways you know not of. *"As the heavens are above the earth, so are my ways above your ways. My ways are not your ways. My thoughts are not your thoughts."*

You could call that a thought form, which is a capacitor to speak, or some people would say it was a fourth-dimensional being. Either way, he was capable of giving directions. He said, "I was not asleep. I was consciously aware, and I heard the voice, and it was all real." That has happened more than once.

This doctor's science, philosophy, and his nominal religious belief could not rescue him, but there is a spirit in man, and the breath of the Almighty hath given him life. He experienced it. You can't take away that experience from him. He tasted the Lord and found Him good. So these truths, you see, were incorporated in his soul.

•   •   •

In the Book of Daniel, it says, *"Thy God whom thou service continually, He will deliver thee."* That's in the sixth chapter of Daniel. The story of Daniel is the story of all men everywhere. It is a story about you. It is said that Daniel while in the lion's den turned his back on the beast and turned toward the light within. The lions were powerless to hurt him. Understanding this drama enables you to extricate yourself from that acute problem in your life.

I remember a soldier telling me that bullets were all around him, coming in all directions, and he said, "The only thing I could remember was a prayer on my mother's knee. 'The Lord is my shepherd, I shall not want.' I didn't even know the meaning of it, but, I had a few verses. '*The Lord is my shepherd, I shall not want. He maketh me to lie down in green pastures. He restoreth my soul.*'"

These few words he remembered, and in his extremity he turned to this power. All of a sudden lightning came and a terrific storm. The rain came down in torrents, and the bullets ceased, and he found his way to safety. There was an answer, a response from an infinite intelligence.

Remember, Daniel is yourself. When faced with a threatening situation, he turned his back on the lions, and he looked for a solution, a way out through the power of the Almighty within him.

For many people when they have a problem, they look at the problem itself. They argue about it, talk about it, magnify it exceedingly in their life, and it engulfs them. Turn away like Daniel from your problem. Contemplate the solution through the power of the Almighty. Focus your attention upon it, and as you do, the power of the Almighty will respond.

Lions in the Bible as mentioned here and in the 91st Psalm represent seemingly insoluble situations of a threatening nature. Yet in every problem lies a solution. In every question, there is an answer. Turn away from the problem. Focus your attention on the solution by claiming and feeling the reality of your desire.

Continue in this belief knowing that an Almighty power is moving on your behalf. *"None shall stay His hand and say unto Him, what doest thou?"*

The realization of your desire is like dropping a seed into the prepared soil in your garden. Your desire for freedom from your problem is a seed you deposit in your subconscious mind, confident that it shall appear in its full-blown potential, as all seeds grow after their kind. Do not worry or be anxious about the way the answer comes, as the ways of your subconscious are past finding out. Your consciousness or awareness is the only presence and power, the eternal cause of all creation.

Create a new Heaven, a new mental attitude, and a new earth will appear. For remember, God is an ever-present help in times of trouble, and you dwell in the secret place. You abide in the shadow of the Almighty, and you say of the Lord, *"He's my refuge, my fortress, my God in Him will I trust."*

He covers you with His feathers, and under His wing shall you rest, and the truth of God shall be your shield and also your butler. Because you set His love upon you, He will prepare a place for you in the homeland of eternity and guide you to safety.

Remember these words, the fourth-dimensional words: *"Thou art my hiding place. Thou shalt preserve me; thou shalt compass me about with songs of deliverance now and forever more."*

The Wonderful Power of Decision

All successful men and women possess one outstanding characteristic, and that is their ability to make prompt decisions, and to persist in carrying those decisions through to completion. A distinguished industrialist once told me that in his fifty years experience in dealing with men and women in the commercial industrial fields, he found that all those who failed had one characteristic in common. It was that they hesitated to make decisions. They vacillated and wavered. Furthermore, when they did make decisions, they were not persistent in adhering to those decisions.

The power to decide and to choose is the foremost quality and the highest prerogative of man. Man's capacity to choose and to initiate what is chosen reveals his power to create as a son of the infinite.

I had a letter from a young man dramatizing the power of decision. He came to a clear-cut decision in his mind, knowing that an Almighty power would back it up. He wanted a Volkswagen automobile, knowing that as he decreed it with feeling, his deeper mind would respond in ways he knew not of. This is what he said:

> "I came to a decision to purchase a car. I did not have the required amount of money. I decided to trust my deeper mind, and I dismissed the problem from my mind knowing my subconscious had the answer. On April 8, a Friday night, a friend asked me if I would go to a teenagers' fair, and I decided to go. A car was being given away that night, and I had a chance of 35,000 to 1 to win. My name was selected, and I won the dream car in my mind, a Volkswagen. I know the reason I got the car was my trust in faith and my deeper mind to solve the problem of a car, for a car is an idea.
>
> "As I continued to use the truths of the infinite, my life is now in complete harmony. I would like to thank you for opening my eyes to this supreme power. Seeing you each Sunday gives me what I need to go through the week. Your thoughts and words are giving me and my family a better life."

A young woman once told me that she felt lonesome, baffled and frustrated because she couldn't decide whether or not she should marry. Can you imagine that? Her mother was very domineering and objected to every young man in whom she was interested. This young woman had lost all initiative and power of decision, with resultant loneliness, frustration, misery, and thralldom. In other words, she put herself in the house of bondage.

At my suggestion, she began to make one decision after another, whereas previously her mother had made all decisions for her. She decided to get an apartment for herself, purchase her own clothes, buy her own shoes, and she decided to furnish the apartment the way she wanted it. She came to a decision to paint the apartment in the way she wanted as well, without asking anybody. She decided to take up dancing, swimming, and golf. She got into the habit of making all decisions for herself.

She finally decided to marry a wonderful man without consulting her mother or anybody else, but just following the dictates of her own heart. She discovered that it's never too late to start making decisions and to live your own life in a wonderful way.

Remember, it is never too late to bring order to a disordered mind or to disordered affairs by coming to logical decisions and letting those decisions stand.

The following letter shows the faith of a woman in her own mental process and in her ability to decide and stick to her decision, knowing that her mind is one with the infinite mind. For there's only one mind common to all individual men.

She said,

"A few years ago, I had a serious automobile accident. The doctor said he had never seen a neck and back broken in so many places, and he doubted I would live. I came to a decision where I decided I would live and be healed by the power of the infinite which made me. I knew all the power of the Godhead would respond to my decision, as I had heard you say many times, that it is done unto you according to your decision. I asked for Prayer Ministry, and I claimed frequently that the infinite healing power was making me whole and perfect, and a marvelous healing followed.

"I had been told that I would have to wear a body and neck brace for several months and perhaps a year. I wore the brace only a few weeks, and now there is nothing wrong with my neck and back. My heart is full of gratitude. I know it is done unto you according to your decision. I decided to be healed, and the infinite healing presence responded accordingly."

As I was talking one day with a prominent pharmacist, he mentioned that life, with its business and professional complications and its attendant confusion, often makes decisions difficult. But he had mastered what he believed to be the ideal method of arriving at the right decision and the correct thing to do.

He said that his favorite Biblical quotation is, *"Be still, and know that I am God."* That's from the 46th Psalm. Then, he added,

> "I dwell in the fact that God or infinite intelligence indwells me, and I focus all my attention on the infinite presence within me. I imagine that the infinite is answering me. I relax and let go completely and feel myself surrounded by the love and the light of the infinite. I also feel myself immersed in God's quietness and stillness. Inwardly, as clear as a crystal, the answer pops into my mind, and it is always right for the occasion."

This pharmacist has evolved a wonderful technique for receiving answers to problems and for coming to the right decisions, with the infinite power within him. Thomas Carlyle once said, "Silence is the element in which great things fashion themselves."

This is a prayer which I have given to thousands of men and women for guidance in making decisions. They have received marvelous results and have been blessed in all their decisions.

"Whatever I need to know comes to me from the infinite presence within. Infinite intelligence is operating through me, revealing to me what I need to know. I radiate love, peace, and goodwill to all mankind in thought, word, and deed. I know that what I send out comes back to me a thousand-fold. God in me knows the answer.

"The perfect answer is made known to me now, for God is the eternal now, and now is the day of salvation, and now is the accepted time. Infinite intelligence and divine wisdom make all decisions through me, and there is only right action and right decision taking place in my life. I wrap myself in the mantle of that infinite ocean of love, and I know divine right decision is mine now.

"I am at peace. I walk in the light, full of faith and confidence and trust in the only power there is. I recognize the lead which comes into my conscious, reasoning mind. It is impossible for me to miss it. God speaks to me in peace, not in confusion. Thank you, Father, for the answer now."

Whenever you are wondering what to do or say, or what decision to make, sit quietly and affirm the above truths which I just enunciated. Do this slowly, quietly, reverently, and with feeling. Do this three times a day in a relaxed, peaceful mood, and you will receive the divine impulse. You will experience the inner, silent knowing of the soul whereby you know that you know.

Sometimes the answer comes as an inner feeling of certitude, a predominant hunch, or a spontaneous idea which wells up clearly in your mind, like toast pops out of the toaster. Intuitively, you will recognize the right answer, the right decision to make. Make right decisions by creative and intelligent prayer, as prayer is realizing there is an infinite intelligence that responds to you.

When you call upon it, it answers you. "*Ask, and you shall receive. Seek, and you shall find. Knock, and it shall be opened to you.*"

"*If you ask for bread, you shall not receive a stone,*" meaning you get the embodiment of the ideal you requested.

When you use the word "logical," you mean that your judgment is reasonable, sound, and valid. This is based on the rational principle of the universe, or the way a thing is, that which is consistent and deducible.

It is logical for you to think good, since only good can follow. It is illogical for you to think evil and to expect good, as seeds or thoughts grow after their own kind. This is a mental and spiritual universe, and the mental law is always supreme. Logical decisions are always based upon the infinite wisdom which guides the planets in their course and causes the sun to shine.

• • •

A saleslady in one of the department stores in Los Angeles was interested in the stock market and had become a very successful investor. This young woman took a required course at night which qualified her for employment in a brokerage house. She had numerous interviews but wasn't able to get employment, and she said it was because of her gender. She said to me, "They just don't want women."

I suggested that she come to a decision and affirm boldly, "I am now employed in a brokerage firm with a marvelous income, consistent with integrity and justice."

I explained to her that the minute she came to a decision in her mind and persisted in that decision, her subconscious mind would respond and open up the way by revealing the perfect plan for fulfillment of her ideal. I instructed her to also follow the lead which would come to her conscious, reasoning mind. It's impossible to miss it.

The sequel is interesting. A strong urge came to her to advertise in the local newspaper, offering to work free for two months, pointing out that she had a large circle of friends as potential customers. She had immediate offers from three firms, one of which she accepted. This shows that you must have faith in your ability to decide, and when you come to a clear-cut decision backed by faith in the powers of your subconscious mind, wonders will happen in your life and you will banish all frustration.

People who fear to make decisions or who are afraid to make choices are actually refusing to recognize their own divinity, for the infinite indwells all men. It is your divine and cosmic right to choose and to make decisions.

You can decide to be healthy, happy, prosperous, and successful because you have dominion over your world. Your subconscious mind is subject to the decrees of our conscious mind, and whatever you decree shall come to pass. The Bible says, "*Whatsoever a man soweth,*" in his subconscious mind, "*so also shall he reap.*" He shall reap it on the screen of space as form, function, experience, and events.

The law of your subconscious mind plays no favorites, no more so than any other law of nature. It is illogical to put your hand on a hot stove. If you do, you will suffer the consequences. To jump off the roof of a high building is illogical, as the law of gravity is impersonal and not vindictive in any way. It is illogical to believe that two and two make five. It is foolish to go against the laws of nature, the immutable rules of the universe, the way things are. It's illogical to steal, because you're impoverishing yourself. You're attracting lack and limitation to yourself and building more misery in your life.

A man once said to me, "I don't know what to do or what is reasonable or logical, and I won't make a decision." I explained to him that he had made a decision. He had decided not to decide. Isn't that a very foolish decision? Isn't that illogical, unreasonable, unscientific? Of course it is.

He had decided not to decide, which meant that he had decided to take what comes from the mass mind, or the law of averages, in which we are all immersed. It is a very negative mind. And if he decided not to decide, the random mind would decide for him, inasmuch as he refused to govern his own.

If you refuse to make a decision, you're going to let circumstances and conditions make a decision for you. Should it be your mother-in-law, or your father-in-law? Who is going to make a decision for you? If you don't think for yourself, perhaps the thought of someone else is thinking in you, or perhaps the mass mind is thinking in you. Because if you don't choose your own thoughts, the mass mind or the law of averages will choose your thoughts for you.

If there's any fear or worry or anxiety in your thinking, you are not thinking at all. It's the mass mind or the law of averages thinking in you, because true thinking is free from fear, free from anxiety. You're like an engineer. You're thinking from the stand-point of principles, eternal verities, eternal truths. Your thoughts are constructive. You're a straight-line thinker.

So this man began to perceive that it was foolish for him not to do his own thinking, reasoning, and deducing, thereby permitting the law of averages or mass thinking to make decisions for him. The mass mind is full of fear, full of hate, jealousy, envy. There is some good in it, but most of it is highly negative. They believe in tragedies and misfortunes of all kinds.

Surely if you don't do your own thinking, some-one else is going to do your thinking for you, and it's not going to be very good. If you don't choose your own emotions, who's going to choose them for you?

So this man reversed his attitude and asserted positively,

"I believe in my power, my ability, and the integ-rity of my own mental and spiritual processes, and I ask myself, 'If I were God, what decision would I make?' I know my motive is right, and my desire is to do the right thing. All my decisions are based upon the fact that infinite wisdom is making all decisions through me, and therefore it must be right action."

Following this prayer, this man has made all his own business, professional, and family decisions, and he is leading a glorious and wonderful life. He has better health, increased efficiency, more love, more understanding, and prosperity along all lines.

The infinite power backs up all your decisions. You are a self-conscious individual, and you have the capacity to decide. It is wrong to let others decide for you or to say, "I will let God decide for me." When you say that, you mean a God outside yourself, a man up in the sky somewhere.

The only way God or infinite intelligence will work for you is through you, your own thoughts, your own imagery, your own decision. The God presence has done everything for you. It has created you and the universe. It gave you a conscious and subconscious mind. It gave you itself, because the infinite or supreme intelligence, which is the presence of God, is within your subconscious depths and you're here to use it. You contact it through the medium of your own thought.

The infinite intelligence will work for you. It will work through you, through your own thought. In order for the Universal to act on the individual plane, it must become the individual.

As Judge Troward points out, in his inimitable textbooks, "The Universal will do nothing for you except through the particular." It must become the particular in order to act it.

You are here to choose. You have volition and initiative. This is why you are an individual. Accept your divinity now and your responsibility, and make decisions for yourself. The other does not know best. When you refuse to make decisions for yourself, you are actually rejecting your divinity, and you are thinking from the standpoint of weakness and inferiority, just like a slave and an underling.

Acknowledge your divinity. You're a choosing, volitional being. You're here to choose. *"Choose ye this day whom you will serve."* Choose whatsoever things are true, whatsoever things are lovely, whatsoever things are just, whatsoever things are pure, and whatsoever things are honest and of good report. Choose these thoughts. Decide to enthrone these thoughts in your mind, and stick to that decision.

A confirmed alcoholic told me that a man once pointed a gun at his temple and told him he would shoot him through the head if he drank the whiskey in front of him. He said, "I had to drink it. I couldn't stop. It was a compulsive act. I didn't care whether or not he shot me."

That shows you he had tremendous power. All the power of the infinite was behind that decision. There's only one power, and all the power of the infinite was behind that decision. He experienced according to his decision.

He subsequently reversed this decision, and at my suggestion declared solemnly for about ten minutes:

"I have come to a definite conclusion in my mind, and my decision is that I am free from this curse of alcoholism. Through the infinite power which backs up this decision, I am completely free. I have peace of mind and sobriety, and I give thanks to the infinite now."

This man has not touched any intoxicating beverages in over five years and is now completely free of the habit. He is a new man. *"Be ye transformed by the renewal of your mind, that ye may approve what is that good and acceptable and perfect will of God."*

"Man shall decree a thing, and it shall come to pass, and the light shall shine upon him." He came to a decision, and he meant it. The power was not in the bottle—the power was within him, and therefore all the power of the infinite is behind your decision. Therefore, *"Choose ye this day whom you will serve."*

God is infinite, and infinity cannot be divided or multiplied. The Bible says, *"I form the light, I create darkness. I make peace, and I create evil. I, the Lord, do all these things."*

The Bible quotation dramatizes and portrays lucidly there's but one power you can use to give you light. This means that when called upon consciously by you, infinite intelligence will cast light on any problem. All that's required is that you come to a clear-cut decision in your mind.

You create darkness when you say, "I'm stymied. I'm blocked. There's no way out." That's a foolish decision. The infinite knows the way. It only knows the answer by your conscious decree, saying, "There's no way out. I'm stymied. It's hopeless." That's your decision. It's the wrong one. It's illogical, unreasonable, unscientific. It's foolish.

By your conscious decree, when you have adopted this mental attitude you're saying infinite intelligence does not know the way out, and according to your decision, you'll live in the darkness and confusion created by your ignorance, your misuse of the law, failure to come to the right decision.

You create peace by dwelling mentally in whatsoever things are true, lovely, noble, and Godlike. You create evil in your experience by thinking negatively, viciously, and destructively. In other words, ask yourself this question. "How am I using this power? What kind of a decision have I arrived at?"

Decide that you're going to use the power constructively, harmoniously, and according to its nature.

You will then call it "God in action." When you use it destructively, negatively, and contrary to its nature, men call it Satan, the devil, misery, suffering and pain and aches and so forth. There is a wonderful power within you. Learn how to use it.

·   ·   ·

Last year, I interviewed a man who had gone bankrupt a short time previously, and had subsequently developed ulcers and high blood pressure. He believed there was a curse following him, that God was punishing him for his past sins, that God had it in for him and that he was now reaping his just deserts.

All these were false beliefs in his mind. I explained to him that as long as he believed there was a jinx following him he would continue to suffer, for the simple reason that man's beliefs take form as experiences, conditions, and events. I told him he had to come to a clear-cut decision, a definite decision in his mind that there was only one power, and that power was moving as unity, as harmony, as peace, as love, and the tendency of life is to heal and restore.

Therefore he came to this decision:

"There is but one Creator, one presence, one power. This power is within me as my mind and spirit. This presence moves through me as harmony, health, and peace. I think, speak, and act from the standpoint of infinite intelligence. I know that thoughts are things. What I feel I attract; what I imagine I become. I constantly dwell on these truths.

"I have come to a clear-cut decision that divine right action governs my life. Divine law and order reign supreme and operate in all phases of my life. Divine guidance is mine. Divine success is mine. Divine prosperity is mine. Divine love fills my soul. Divine wisdom governs all my transactions.

"Whenever fear or worry come into my mind, I affirm immediately, 'God is guiding me now, or God knows the answer.' I make a habit of this, and I know that miracles are happening in my life."

He prayed out loud in this manner five or six times daily. At the end of a month, his health was restored, and he was taken in as a partner at a growing firm.

He came to a decision, and his whole life had been transformed. There was only one power, and that power was moving as unity, as harmony, as health and peace. There are no divisions or quarrels in that power, nothing to oppose it, thwart it, vitiate it, or interfere with it. The new idea—the new decision arrived at in his mind—became his master and compelled him to express the riches of life.

Ideas are our masters. According to our decision, is it done unto us. Enthrone in your mind divine ideas, and watch the wonders that happen as you pray.

There's a wonderful power within you. Begin to use it now. It's the Almighty power, the one alone who lives in the hearts of all men. The Bible says, *"Let your words be yea, yea, and no, no. Anything more than this is evil."*

Say yes. Come to a decision. Say yes to all ideas and truths which heal, bless, inspire, elevate, and dignify your soul. Say no, definitely, positively, and absolutely, to all negative thoughts, to anything that would instill fear into your mind, that would drag you down, that would create doubt in your mind. Reject all these suggestions as unfit for the house of God.

These two words, yes and no, come to a decision about them. Say yes to health, to happiness, to peace, to the abundant life. Say no to sickness, to misery and suffering and lack. Reject these ideas. Reject any suggestion or any thought that does not fill your soul with joy. Reject any suggestion that does not give you more confidence and more faith in yourself.

*   *   *

"Don't put off until tomorrow what you can do today" is an old saying. "Procrastination is the thief of time" is another. If you're putting it off, wondering what I shall do and when I'm going to decide, maybe next week, you'll become misery. You'll become neurotic, frustrated, unhappy. You're placing yourself in bondage.

If your motivation is good, if it looks good to you, come to a decision. It's far better to do something right now than do nothing. *"For as a man thinketh in his heart, so is he."* The heart is your subconscious mind, the seat of your emotions and feelings. Whatever thought or image you have in your mind now, your feeling nature, that's the spirit within you, and it begins to flow through that matrix.

Your thought and feeling create your destiny. Your thought and feeling create everything in your life, mold and fashion your destiny. Whatever you think and feel to be true comes to pass. Come to a decision—now.

A man said to me that he was offered two positions. They both looked good to him, and someone was going to call him up at 2:00 and wanted an answer. He said, "I have no particular feeling about either one of them. They both look good. They're about the same."

I said, "When the man calls at 2:00, and you have no ulterior motives, and it looks good to you, pronounce it good. Whatever you say to him, the first thought that comes to you when he calls up—yes or no—will be right."

I said, "When your motivation is right and things look good to you, what on earth are you afraid of? There's a principle of right action. There's no principle of wrong action. Therefore, you pronounce it good."

He said yes, and it turned out to be good. He pronounced it good.

●　　●　　●

I talked to a man in a hotel in Tokyo a few years ago. He was 90 years of age, he was on crutches, and he was an American. We talked for quite a while, and he said, "You know, when I was 60 years of age, I wanted to go around the world. I wanted to take my wife on a trip around the world. But I postponed it. I said 'I'll wait until my daughter grows up or gets married.' Now, I'm crippled with arthritis, and I can't take that trip."

He postponed it, and didn't give himself or his wife the joy of that trip. He refused to come to a decision, postponing it till his daughter grew up and got married. All of that was nonsense. Your good is right now. You don't wait for anything. You take it now, because a trip around the world has nothing to do with your daughter getting married or remaining single—nothing at all.

It has to do with *you*. Make up your mind. Come to a clear-cut decision, and if your motivation is right, that decision is right. It's God in action right now.

You're claiming divine law and order in your life. Claiming divine right action in your life. Divine law and order means that the law of harmony, beauty, love, peace, and abundance are operating in your subconscious, rather than man-made laws, rather than creeds and dogmas and tradition. It also means you're expressing yourself at your highest level. You're releasing your hidden talents in a wonderful way, with integrity and honesty.

It also means you're receiving marvelous and wonderful compensation, because the money you need when you want to use it should be there, available and in circulation. When you're able to do what you want to do, when you want to do it, you're as rich as Croesus. That's divine law and order.

If you can't buy your wife a new car when she needs one, that's not divine law and order. There's something frightfully wrong. There's a principle of right action. There's no principle of wrong action.

When you hear a person saying, "Maybe I did something wrong," turn around and believe there's a principle of right action, like the wheels in your automobile have to be round. If they're not round, you'll kill yourself. That's right action.

Claim that you're under the shadow of the Almighty. *"I will say of the Lord, he's my refuge, my fortress. My God, in Him will I trust."* Isn't that a wonderful prayer for guidance and right action, your 91st Psalm? "I dwell in the secret place." That's your own mind where you walk and talk with God.

"I abide in the shadow of the Almighty, I'll say of the Lord, the Lordly power. He's my refuge, my fortress. My God, in Him will I trust. He covers me with His feathers, and under his wing shall I rest."

Why then, should you worry or be fearful about doing the right thing? You're under a guiding principle, and the angels, you're told, will watch over you. Angels are intelligence and wisdom, the creative ideas that well up within you.

Thus you're guided to your true place, to do the right thing, for the highest and the best begins to move through you. Put God first in your life. God is the supreme intelligence which started your heartbeat. It governs all the vital organs. It watches over you. Its tendency is to heal and restore.

"Choose ye this day whom you will serve." Choose harmony, choose right action, choose beauty, choose abundance, choose security in your life. Choose these things because the higher self is God, and that Almighty power will move on your behalf. But you must turn to it. *"Call upon me, and I will answer you."*

Decide with your mind, not with your emotions. There's a man who got mad at the boss. He was full of bitterness and hostility, so he told the boss off, and quit in a huff. Then he took another job and said to me, "I have more problems in this job than I had in the previous one."

He realized his decision was wrong. He made a decision on the basis of anger, resentment, and hostility—his emotions. He was carried away by his emotions. You must make decisions based upon true judgment, upon wisdom and understanding. Reason the thing out. Study the pros and cons and be rational and reasonable.

Make a decision on the basis of factual rationality. Reason the thing out. Does it seem reasonable and logical to you? Assemble the facts together. Get all the data you can, and try and solve it objectively.

Use no mental coercion, no force. Don't grit your teeth and clench your fists. Don't say, "I must get an answer at a certain time," or, "The judge must give me a decision on the 15th of April." That's nonsense.

Do everything you can, objectively, quietly, with faith and with confidence. You'll feel good about it, and if the situation looks good to you, the investment or whatever it is, then go ahead and do it.

Always remember, if your motivation is right and you're praying for guidance and right action, and something looks good to you, go ahead and say, "It's God in action." Pronounce it good. Why should you hesitate? Why should you vacillate and waver? Why become a neurotic? Why become frustrated? Come to a decision, and quickly.

The clear impression comes to you when someone calls you on the phone and says, "I must have an answer now. I'm on the phone." If you have been praying about it and thinking about it, whatever you say will be right.

Empty out all preconceived notions. A man said to me one time, "Do you think I've arrived at the right decision?"

"Well," I said to him, "is it based upon the Golden Rule and the law of love?" Then he got red in the face, and I said, "You answered your own question. If your decision is to take advantage of someone, pull the wool over somebody's eyes, or cheat him, whatever decision you'd arrived at in such a case would be wrong because to hurt the other is to hurt yourself. So is your decision based upon the Golden Rule and the law of love?"

Love is wishing for everyone what you wish for yourself. When you love another, you love to see the other become and express all they long to become and express. There are women I talk to, forty and fifty years of age, where their mother made all the decisions for them. When you allow that, you're robbing yourself of your own initiative, your own experience, your own divinity, because the God presence is within you. *"I said, ye are gods, and all of you are sons of the most high."*

You're here to choose, to mold and fashion your own destiny. Learn to make decisions. Start now. After you're seven or eight years of age, you should begin to learn to make decisions to some degree, with supervision of course. When you're 18 years of age you should make your own decisions, move out of your parents' home and establish your own apartment, roll up your sleeves, and get busy. Learn to make decisions. Exercise your initiative.

One man said, "When I'm confused and mixed up a little bit, and I'm unsure, I pray about it, and sometimes I flip a coin. But I know that any kind of action is better than inaction, so I come to a decision."

If you're going on the road to San Francisco and you're on the wrong road, some man stops you and he says, "Turn to the right. That's the right road." Now you're right, aren't you? You're on the right road. You made a mistake, so what? Everybody makes mistakes.

When you went to school, didn't you make hundreds of them? That's why you had a rubber eraser on the end of your pencil. Everybody, including Mother and Father, knew you'd make mistakes.

As you continue to make decisions, you'll have a new zest and a new thrill. Things are not in the saddle. Circumstances can't create circumstances. Conditions are not created. There are no powers outside you. You don't give power to a created thing. You do not give power to the phenomenalistic world. You give power to the Creator, and that's the supreme intelligence within you.

Avoid indecisiveness, which attends much religious prayer. People say, "Is it right for me to pray for wealth?" How absurd, how ridiculous. Is it right for me to pray for success? Maybe God doesn't want me to succeed. That is stupidity, jungle philosophy. It is too stupid for words.

Does God want me to sing? Well, if God gave you a voice, he wants you to sing. The singing capacity is within you. If you're able to sing, and that quality is within you, go ahead and sing. You don't wait for God to sing. God will sing through you, but God is the only presence and power.

If you have the desire to paint, go ahead and paint. If you love animals, or if you'd love to be a chemist or something, or a musician, go ahead, and follow the lead which comes to you.

People say, "Is it right that I should pray for a car?" What is a car? An idea in the mind of God. That's all a car is, the spirit of God made manifest. It's God outside your door taking the form of a car, for there's only God. There's nothing else but God.

God is spirit, and the grass is God, too. The clothes you wear is God. God and goods are synonymous. You go into a store and you say, "Goods." Well, what are you talking about? God and good are the same.

The goods are spirit made manifest. The apple on a tree is spirit made manifest.

There's only spirit. Everything is made inside and out of it. The material world is spirit made manifest. Everything you touch is the spirit made manifest.

Questions such as "Is it right for me to get married?" are absurd. They're based on superstition, ignorance, and fear. Such questions as these rob the mind of decision and force.

If you pray for guidance, a higher form of prayer, you will overcome your theological concepts because your higher self will teach you as you go along. The spirit of truth will lead you to all truths. You say, "God is guiding me now. Right action reigns supreme. The spirit of truth leads me to all truth."

You've come to a marvelous decision. Be definite. Have goals. Announce purposes. Your receipts will be offset by your liabilities. As in all business, your prayer is answered to the level of your belief. Your consciousness is what you know consciously and subconsciously.

If you pray for prosperity, success, achievement, and victory, say, "Come to a decision." Say, "Prosperity is mine now. I'm going to be wealthy. I'm going to have all the wealth I need to do what I want to do when I want to do it." Your subconscious will respond, and the answer will be filtered through your present state of mind.

Raise your sights, and you'll go where your vision is. You know merchants in the East do that, Egypt and other places. They set the price very high. The tourist comes in and he's supposed to bargain. They'll come down, there will be several markdowns, yet they'll still make a profit.

With negative beliefs in your mind, like if you're praying for prosperity, success, and achievement, but you're jealous of others, their promotion or the six cars in their garage, or the million dollars they have, then that negation, that resentment, that envy, that jealousy blocks your good, inhibits your growth and interferes with your prosperity.

Frederick the Great collected a lot of money, or at least his agents did, and he said, "What happens to all the money we collect?"

It was a hot day, and the members of his cabinet were around the table. There was a bowl of ice there and some water with some ice in it. One man took up a little piece of the ice, and passed it around in men's hands. When it got to the king, it was a very small piece. He said, "That, Sire, is the answer."

So if you are down on yourself, or you're jealous or envious of others, you are inhibiting the flow of that infinite ocean of riches through you. Therefore wish for everyone what you wish for yourself, for love is the fulfilling of the law, and love is goodwill, wishing for everyone what you wish for yourself.

Regrets, remorse, hate, peeves, grudges, looking to externals, giving power to people and conditions and circumstances are negatives of the mind, and they all cut down on the riches of the infinite. Give all your allegiance and devotion.

Let your expectation be from Him who giveth to all life breath, and all things. Get it straight. Come to that decision. Look to the source. Then as you do that, come to the decision that, "From the depths of my heart I wish for every person in the world the riches of the infinite, health and happiness and peace and all the blessings of life." Then watch the flow of vitality and riches to you.

This is what holds so many people back, because they're down on themselves, they're full of remorse, peeves and grudges, and they don't receive healing with that attitude of mind. They don't prosper either.

Real success is a spiritual development. Stop carping on criticism, because that cuts down on the quality of good you receive. *"Exalt God in the midst of you, might He to heal."*

• • •

There is a young boy who steals a bottle of milk. From there he goes on stealing other things, apples, and larger, more valuable items. Eventually the sum total of his choices lands him in jail. The reason the man is in jail is the sum total of his choices. That's all we are.

It's an illogical decision to steal the bottle of milk, because it induces fear. He hopes a policeman isn't looking, so he's doing it with fear and apprehension, also he's impoverishing himself and attracting lack and limitation to himself.

Whenever you make a decision, remember the power of the Almighty backs it up, whether it's false or whether it is good. If it's an illogical decision like the boy stealing a bottle of milk, he's using the power of the infinite against ourselves. There is the power of reason within you.

There's a principle of life. It knows how to protect itself. It's within you. It heals a cut in your finger. It wakes you up if you say I want to wake up at 3:00 in the morning, wakes you up whether there's a clock in the room or not, or whether there's a storm and the clock has stopped.

There's an intelligence within you that governs all your vital organs, your breathing, and so on. It seeks to heal and restore you. The infinite cannot punish you. Life cannot punish, the absolute cannot punish. The law doesn't punish. Man punishes himself by his negative, destructive thinking, by his misuse of law.

A good judge doesn't punish. He just invokes the law. So cease making illogical decisions. Learn the simple truth. *"I said, ye are Gods, and all of you are sons of the most high, and you are the temple of the living God, and the Kingdom of God is within you."*

The infinite wisdom and the infinite power is within you, and if you were God, what decision would you make? You'd make a decision on right action, on harmony, on peace, on love and goodwill. Wouldn't you? You would begin to think, speak, and act from the standpoint of the infinite center, from the infinite power.

You wouldn't make any decisions from the standpoint of some old theologian, or what your grandmother said. You'd say, "There's a guiding principle within me, and I'm going to make decisions according to that guiding principle which is absolute harmony and absolute peace."

"I said, ye are Gods, and all of you are sons of the most high." That God presence is within you, the boundless wisdom, the infinite intelligence. Stop denying your divinity. Your grandmother doesn't know best, and when you want to get married, come to a decision and say, "Infinite intelligence attracts to me the right person"—man or woman—"who harmonizes with me in every way. The deeper currents of my mind bring both of us together."

Trust the infinite intelligence, and don't ask your mother or your grandmother whether you should marry the man or the woman, because then you're denying your own divinity. You're saying, "Look, I can't choose," which of course you can. That's your prerogative.

There's the person who says, "If God had wanted me to be well, he'd heal me." This is a sort of blasphemy, for the tendency of life is always to heal and to restore. When you burn yourself, it proceeds to reduce the edema and gives you new skin and tissue. When you cut yourself, it forms thrombin, builds a bridge across the cut, and seeks to heal you. It kills the germs when they invade your body as well.

"There's one mind common to all individual men," Emerson said, and you're here to make choices. You're an organ of God, and God hath need of you where you are. Otherwise you wouldn't be here. You're here to reproduce all that's true of the infinite.

You can make decisions that are normal, rational, logical, and reasonable. The tendency of life, the will of God for you, is the greatest measure of life, love, truth, and beauty. So it's foolish and rank superstition to say, "If God wanted to heal me, he would heal me." That's blasphemy because you're telling a lie about the infinite. You're lying about the infinite being.

•   •   •

I have seen men and women live together in hate and resentment for many years rather than get a divorce. They said they were thinking in terms of the children, but children grow up in the image and likeness of the dominant mental and emotional climate of the home. The children become delinquents and are sick all the time because the atmosphere of the home is hatred, resentment, hostility, and rage. That's a frightful way to live.

Come to a decision. Realize it's far more decent, honorable, and Godlike to break up a lie than live it. It's a frightful thing to live a lie and contaminate the minds of all those around you. At least you have respect for the woman who got a divorce, more so than the woman who's living a lie for twenty and twenty-five years.

There are people fearful to make a decision, sometimes because of religious, sometimes because of political and financial reasons. Some of them would rather get cancer, tuberculosis, and arthritis than break up a lie. Many people decide every day to do something about it, but then they do nothing at all. All the power of life is within you, enabling you to make your decision right now. It's illogical to live a lie.

I've seen people come to a logical decision. They said, "I will arise and go to my Father." They say, "I will not live this way anymore." It takes two to make a good marriage, or a business partnership prosperous.

If two men are in business, and one is drunk all the time, insulting the customers, the house is divided, and certainly they're going to go broke. The thing for them to do is to dissolve the partnership, bless each other, and make a decision to lead a full and happy life. But it's wrong to live that way. If the two agree to do the right thing and practice the Golden Rule and the law of love, that's a different thing.

Do what you're supposed to do. You're equipped to do it. There's a guiding principle within you. God wants you to be happy. You're here to reproduce all that's true of God. You're here to glorify God and enjoy him forever. That should be your decision.

Your decision should be to lead a full and happy life. God gave you richly all things to enjoy. "God made you rich. Why then are you poor?"

* * *

"I am come that you might have life and have it more abundantly. Heretofore, you ask for nothing. Now ask that your joy might be full." In Him there is fullness of joy. In Him there is no darkness at all.

The power of life is there. There is no such thing as indecision. There is only decision. A person who decides not to decide, then the mass mind makes a decision for them, and their life will be a mess. That mass mind believes in tragedies and difficulties and chaos and misfortune of all kinds. Most of it is highly negative.

Surely you don't want that moving into your mind. If you do not come to a decision every morning to charge your mental and spiritual batteries with Godlike truths, who then will do your thinking for you? Who will govern your emotions? Who will govern your mood? Who's choosing your emotions?

The power and the wisdom of the infinite is within you, and you're here to use it. "*Come to the waters and drink. He that hath no money, ye, let him come. Buy wine and milk without money, without price.*" The price is belief. It's recognition. It's assumption. Assume there's an Almighty power and "Your assumptions," as Churchill said, "harden into facts."

Say you're up in the mountains, fishing, and you've lost your way in the stream. You see an old man of the woods, and you say, "How can I get back to the main road?" He tells you exactly how to go. You follow his directions and you find he's right. You assumed what he said is right, and it hardened into a fact, didn't it?

Likewise, assume there's an infinite intelligence within you. It started your heartbeat, grows hair on your face, digests your food. It watches over you when you're sound asleep. It wakes you up if you suggest particular times when you go to sleep.

If you're seeking an answer to an investment and say, "Infinite intelligence reveals to me the answer about this investment," it seeks to heal you. You may wake up in the morning, and you have a persistent feeling not to touch it. That's the voice of the divine answering you. Don't touch it.

I've talked to hundreds of women who say, "I knew as I was walking up the aisle to marry that man, I shouldn't have done it." There's that lingering feeling they had within them, a sort of hunch, which was the life principle seeking to protect them. They ignored it, rejected it, and eventually they had to get a divorce.

• • •

Follow that thing when it comes, that inner sense of touch. Like the man who prayed about an investment recently in Nevada. He said, "Infinite intelligence is guiding me. It reveals to me and my wife the right thing to do regarding this investment."

He came to a decision that there was a guiding principle. There's no *if*, there's no *and*, there's no *but*. Then, according to that decision, it was done unto him. He had a dream in the middle of the night where he saw these men in prison and a guard with a gun at the door. He woke up, and he knew he was dealing with con men who had served time. Had he invested, he would have lost everything.

You have to come to a decision that there is a guiding principle within you, and wonders will then happen in your life. When you have a difficult decision to make, or when you fail to see the solution to your problem, begin at once to think constructively about it. If you're fearful and worried, you're not really thinking.

True thinking is free from fear. Quiet the mind, still the body. Tell your body to relax, it has to obey you. Your body has no volition, initiative, or self-conscious intelligence. Your body is an emotional disk which records your beliefs and impressions. Mobilize your attention. Focus your thought on the solution to your problem. Try to solve it like a detective does with your conscious mind.

Think how happy you would be about the perfect solution. Get all the information you can. Sense the feeling you would have if the perfect answer were yours now.

Let your mind play with this mood in a relaxed way, and if you're going to sleep, then fall asleep contemplating the answer. If you do not have the answer when you awaken, get busy about something else. Once you are preoccupied with something else, the answer will likely come into your mind like toast pops out of a toaster.

In receiving guidance from your subconscious mind, the simple way is the best. A man lost a valuable ring that was an heirloom. He looked everywhere for it and could not locate it. At night he talked to the subconscious in the same manner that I'm talking to you. He said, prior to dropping off to sleep—talking to his higher self—that there's nothing lost in the infinite.

He said to his higher self, "You know all things. You're all wise. You're omnipresent. You know where that ring is, and you are now revealing to me where it is." That's called prayer. That's coming to a decision. That's not mumbo-jumbo.

In the morning he awoke suddenly with the words ringing in his ear, *"Ask Robert."* Robert happened to be his son. He asked Robert about it, and he said, "I picked it up in the yard while I was playing with the boys and put it on the desk in my room. I didn't think it was worth anything, so I didn't say anything about it."

It only knows the answer. *"When you call upon it, it will answer you. It will be with you in trouble. It will set you on high because you hath known its name. In quietness and in confidence shall it be your strength. It is written He careth for you. God knows only the answer."*

Developing Your Healing Consciousness

Let us dwell upon these great truths of the Bible:

"I am the Lord that healeth thee. If thou return to the Almighty, thou shall be built up. The Lord will perfect that which concerneth me. Behold, I am the Lord, the God of all flesh. Is there anything too hard for me? I will restore health into thee, and I will heal thee of thy wounds, sayeth the Lord. Who healeth all thy disease? Who satisfy thy mouth with good things? Who restored thy youth like an eagle?

"He sent His word and healed them and delivered them from their destruction. I will put my spirit in you, and ye shall live. Thou will keep him in perfect peace whose mind is stayed on thee because he trusted in me. Therefore, I say unto thee what things so ever you desire, when ye pray, believe that ye receive them, and ye shall have them. All things are possible to him that believes it.

"Go thy way; thy faith hath made thee whole. Pray for one another that ye may be healed. The prayer of a fervent, righteous man availeth much. I have heard thy prayer, I have seen thy tears; behold, I will heal thee. A merry heart *maketh a cheerful countenance, a broken spirit drieth the bones. The tongue of the wise is health.*"

And Paul says, "*Glorify God in your body.*"

There is only one healing power. It is called by many names, such as God, infinite healing presence, divine love, divine providence, nature, the miraculous healing power, the life principle, and many others. This knowledge reaches back into the dim recesses of the past.

An inscription has been found written over ancient temples that reads, "The doctor dresses the wound, and God heals it." The healing presence of God is within you. No psychologist, minister, doctor, surgeon, priest, or psychiatrist heals anyone. For example, the surgeon removes a tumor, thereby removing the block and making way for the healing power of God to restore you.

The psychologist or psychiatrist endeavors to remove the mental block and encourages the patient to adopt a new mental attitude that tends to release the healing presence, flowing through the patient as harmony, health, and peace. The minister asks you to forgive yourself and others and get in tune with the infinite while letting the healing power of love, peace, and goodwill flow through your subconscious mind, thereby cleansing all the negative patterns that may be lodged therein.

This infinite healing presence of life has been called the Father in the Bible. It is the healing agent in all diseases, whether mental, emotional, or physical. The miraculous healing power in your subconscious mind is scientifically directed. It can heal your mind, body, affairs of all disease and impediments, when it is scientifically, consciously, and knowingly directed.

This healing power will respond to you regardless of your race, creed, or color. It does not care whether you belong to any church or have any creedal affiliations. You have had hundreds of healings since you were a child. You can recall how this healing presence brought curative results to cuts, burns, bruises, contusions, sprains, and so on. In all probability, you did not aid the healing in any way by the application of external remedies.

*   *   *

A few years ago, a young man from a local university came to see me with the complaint that he was constantly hearing spirit voices, that they made him do nasty things. They would not let him alone. Neither would they permit him to read the Bible or other spiritual books. He was convinced that he was talking to supernatural beings. This young man was *clairaudient*.

Not knowing that all men possess this faculty to some degree, he began to think it was due to evil spirits.

His superstitious beliefs caused him to describe the voices as departed spirits. Through constant worry, he became a monomaniac on the subject. His subconscious mind, dominated and controlled by an all-potent but false suggestion, gradually took over control and mastery of his objective faculties, and his reason abdicated its throne.

He was what you would call mentally unbalanced, as are all men who allow their false beliefs to obtain the ascendancy. I explained to this university student that his subconscious mind is of tremendous importance and significance, and that it can be influenced negatively and positively. He had to make sure that he influenced it only positively, constructively, and harmoniously.

The subconscious mind possesses transcendent powers, but it is at the same time amenable to good and bad suggestions. The explanation that I gave him made a profound impression on him. I gave him the following written prayer, which he was to repeat for 10 or 15 minutes three or four times a day:

"God's love, peace, harmony, and wisdom flood my mind and heart. I love the truth, I hear the truth, and I know the truth. I know God is Love, and His love surrounds me, enfolds me, and enwraps me. God's river of peace floods my mind, and I give thanks for my freedom."

He repeated this prayer slowly, quietly, reverently, and with deep feeling, particularly prior to sleep.

By identifying himself with harmony and peace, he brought about a rearrangement of the thought patterns and imagery in his mind, and a healing followed. He brought about a healing of his mind by repetition of these truths, coupled with faith and expectancy.

My prayer for him was,

"John is thinking rightly. He is reflecting divine wisdom and divine intelligence in all his ways. His mind is the perfect mind of God, unchanging and eternal. He hears the voice of God, which is the inner voice of peace and love. God's river of peace governs his mind, and he's full of wisdom, poise, balance, and understanding. Whatever is vexing him is leaving him now, and I pronounce him free and at peace."

At the end of a week, this young man was completely free and at peace.

* * *

Some time ago, a woman told me that her child had a very high fever and was not expected to live. The doctor had prescribed small doses of aspirin and had administered an antibiotic preparation. The mother was involved in a contemplated divorce suit, was terribly agitated, and emotionally disturbed. This disturbed feeling was communicated subconsciously to the child, and naturally the child became ill.

Children are at the mercy of their parents and are controlled by the dominant mental atmosphere and emotional climate of those around them. They have not yet reached the age of reason when they can take control of their own thoughts, emotions, and reactions to life.

This mother, at my suggestion, decided to become more at ease and relax her tensions by reading the 23rd Psalm, praying for guidance and for the peace and harmony of her husband. She poured out love and goodwill to him and overcame her resentment and inner rage.

The fever of the child was due to the suppressed rage and anger of the mother, which was subjectively felt by the child and expressed as a high fever due to the excitation of the child's mind. Having quieted her own mind, the mother began to pray for the child in this manner:

"Spirit which is God is the life of my child. Spirit has no temperature. It is never sick or feverish. The peace of God flows through my child's mind and body. The harmony, health, love, and perfection of God are made manifest in every atom of my child's body. She is relaxed and at ease, poised, serene, and calm. I am now stirring up the gift of God within her, and all is well."

She repeated the above prayer every hour, for several hours. Shortly thereafter, she noticed a remarkable change in her child, who awakened and asked for a doll and something to eat. The temperature became normal. What had happened? The fever left the little girl because the mother was no longer feverish or agitated in her mind. Her mood of peace, harmony, and love was instantaneously felt by the child, and a corresponding reaction was produced.

We are all natural-born healers for the simple reason that the healing presence of God is within all men, and all of us can contact it with our thoughts. It responds to all. The healing presence is in the dog, the cat, the tree, and the bird. It is omnipresent. It is in the soil. It is the life of all things.

There are different degrees of faith. There is the man who, through faith, heals his ulcers; another who heals a deep-seated, so-called incurable malignancy. It is as easy for the healing presence of God to heal a tubercular lung as it is to heal a cut on your finger or a pimple on your nose.

There is no great or small in the God that made us all. There is no big or little, no hard or easy. Omnipotence is within all men. The prayers of the man who lays his hands on another in order to induce a healing simply appeals to the cooperation of the patient's subconscious, whether the latter knows it or not, whether he ascribes it to divine intercession or not. A response takes place, for according to the patient's belief it is done unto him.

I remember the story in the Bible where the dead man was commanded, and He said to the dead man, "Young man, I say unto thee arise," and he that was dead sat up and began to speak. That's in the book of Luke. When it says the dead man sat up and began to speak, it means that when your prayer is answered, you speak in a new tongue of joyous health, and you exude an inner radiance. Your dead hopes and desires speak when you bear witness to your inner beliefs and assumptions.

As a corollary to this, I would like to tell you about a young man I saw in Ireland a few years ago. He was a distant relative. He was in a comatose condition. His kidneys had not functioned for three days. His condition had been pronounced hopeless. I went to see him accompanied by one of his brothers. I knew that he was a devout Catholic, and I said to him, "Jesus is right here, and you see Him. He's putting His hand out, and at this moment is laying His hand on you, and you are being healed this moment."

I repeated this several times slowly, quietly, and positively. He was unconscious when I spoke, or in a comatose condition, and was not consciously aware of either of us. But he then sat up in bed, opened his eyes, and said to both of us, "Jesus was here. I know I am healed. I shall live."

What had happened? This man's subconscious mind had accepted my statement that Jesus was there, and his subconscious projected that thought form, which he saw in his prayer book or in statues in the church. That is, this man's concept of Jesus was portrayed based upon what he saw in statues, paintings, and so on.

He believed that Jesus was there in the flesh and that he had placed his hands upon him. Remember, whatever suggestion you give to your subconscious mind, it acts upon it, whether true or false.

The readers of my book, *The Power of Your Subconscious Mind,* are well aware of the fact that you can tell a man who is in a trance that his grandfather is here now, and that he will see him clearly. He will see what he believes to be his grandfather based on his subconscious memory picture.

You can give the same man a post-hypnotic suggestion by saying to him, "When you come out of this trance, you will greet your grandfather and talk to him," and he will do exactly that. This is called a subjective hallucination. The faith that was kindled in the subconscious of my Catholic relative, based on his firm belief that Jesus came to heal him, was the healing factor.

It is always done unto us according to our faith, mental conviction, or just blind belief. His subconscious mind was amenable to my suggestion; his deeper mind received and acted upon the idea I had implanted in his mind. In a sense, you could call such an incident the resurrection of the dead. It was the resurrection of his health and vitality, and according to his belief it was done unto him.

True faith is based on the knowledge of the way your conscious and subconscious minds function, and on the combined harmonious functioning of these two levels of mind scientifically directed. Blind faith is healing without any scientific understanding whatsoever of the forces involved.

The voodoo doctor or witch doctor in the jungles of Africa heals by faith. So do the bones of dogs believed to be the bones of saints by the believer or anything else that moves man's mind from fear to faith. In all instances, regardless of the technique, modus operandi, process, incantation, or invocation offered to saints and spirits, it is the subconscious mind that does the healing. Whatever you believe is operative instantly in your subconscious mind. This is the law of mind.

Be like the little eight-year-old boy in Sunday school. Eye drops were not clearing up his eye infection, and he prayed as follows. "God, you made my eyes. I demand action, I want healing now. Hurry up. Thank you." He had a remarkable healing because of his simplicity, spontaneity, and childlike faith in God. *"Go, thou, and do likewise."*

Don't let the word *incurable* frighten you. Realize that you are dealing with the creative intelligence which made your body and that although some men will say that a healing is impossible, be assured that this infinite healing presence is instantly available.

You can always draw on its power through the creative law of your own mind. Make use of this power now and perform miracles in your life. Remember that a miracle cannot prove that which is impossible. It is a confirmation of that which is possible. *"With God all things are possible. I will restore health unto thee, and I will heal thee of thy wounds, sayeth the Lord."* That's in Jeremiah.

•   •   •

The word Lord in the Bible means the creative law of your mind. There is a deep-lying, healing principle which permeates the entire universe, that flows through your mental patterns, images, and choices and objectifies them in form. You can bring into your life anything you wish through this infinite healing presence, which operates through your own mind.

Millions of Christians and Jews are atheists because they say oft times, "My body is incurable. It's hopeless. I can't be healed." At the same time, they say, "With God all things are possible." They say that infinite healing presence that made the body, that infinite intelligence which made it, can't heal it.

It is just the same as if you made an ice box and told me that you couldn't fix it when it was out of order. I wouldn't believe you. Nobody would.

When you deny the infinite healing presence, you're an atheist. It created the body, and it certainly can heal it. It knows all the processes and functions of the body. It made it from a cell. Surely, *"He that hath made the eye, can he not see? He that hath made the ear, can he not hear?"*

You may use this healing presence for any purpose. It is not confined to healing of the body or mind. It is the same principle which attracts to you the ideal husband or wife, prospers you in business, finds for you your true place in life, and reveals answers to your most difficult problems.

Through the correct application of this principle, you can become a great salesman, musician, physician, or surgeon. You can use it to bring harmony where there's discord, peace to supplant pain, joy in place of sadness, and abundance in place of poverty.

The first step in healing is not to be afraid of the manifest condition from this very moment. The second step is to realize that the condition is only the product of past thinking, which will have no more power to continue its existence. The third step is to mentally exalt the miraculous healing power of God within you.

This procedure will instantly stop the production of all mental poisons in you, or in the person for whom you are praying. Live in the embodiment of your desire, and your thought and feeling will soon be made manifest. Do not allow yourself to be swayed by human opinion and worldly fears, but live emotionally in the belief that it is God in action in your mind and body.

•   •   •

The Bible says, "Heal the sick, cleanse the lepers, cast out devils, raise the dead, freely ye have received, freely ye give." The word "heal" is an Old English word meaning to make whole, to integrate, to unite. Ill health is the lack of oneness with God. It means separation from the divine.

"He restoreth my soul," the Psalm says. Your soul is your subconscious mind. You can restore your subconscious mind to wholeness, beauty, peace, and serenity. Fill your conscious mind with life-giving patterns. Fill your mind with harmony, health, peace, wholeness, beauty, right action. Think from principles such as harmony, peace, beauty, love, joy.

Preach "the Kingdom of Heaven is at hand." You much preach it first to yourself, that the kingdom of intelligence, wisdom, and power, the boundless love, the infinite intelligence of God, are locked in your subconscious mind.

Teach that to your own faculties of mind. Teach your faculties of mind to give up their illusions, false beliefs, ill will, resentment, antagonism. You can't be healed and at the same time resent and hate and be full of self-condemnation. It's impossible.

You must give up all of these false beliefs and accept that the spirit is God. Wish for everyone what you wish for yourself: health, happiness, peace, and all the blessings of life. Forgive yourself for harboring negative thoughts. Forgive everybody. You then create a vacuum, and the Holy Spirit of God will rush in and heal you.

Accept that the spirit in you is God. It's the only cause, and you do not give power to externals. You do not give power to the atmosphere, the winds, or the waves, or to germs, or to anything. Change your mind, and you change your body. Be transformed by the renewal of your mind.

Fill your mind with the truths of God, and you will empty your mind of everything unlike God, just like a pail of dirty water. If you have patience, and you *drip, drip, drip* clean water into it, after a while you and I can drink out of that pail of water.

Likewise, when you fill your mind with the eternal verities, whatsoever things are true, lovely, noble, and Godlike, you will expunge and obliterate from your deeper mind everything unlike God, and healing will take place because thousands of cells are dying every second, and as you fill your mind with that which is lovely, noble, and Godlike, then the tissues and the nerves and the cells will take on a spiritual overtone.

Like spiritual penicillin, you will destroy the bacteria, fear, worry, and anxiety. Persistence and repetition work miracles in your mind. Reiterate the great truths such as, *"The healing power of God is now flowing through me, healing me and making me whole. The infinite healing presence made me. It knows how to heal. It knows all the processes and functions of my body, and I claim that the Holy Spirit is flowing through me now animating, sustaining, healing, and restoring my whole being to wholeness, beauty, and perfection."*

This presence and power is flowing through you now, healing, vitalizing, and restoring your soul because your soul is your subconscious mind. No matter what the problem is, no matter what the difficulty is, it is a negative pattern, a complex and poisoned pattern lodged in the recesses of your subconscious mind, and the law is subject to the higher. Therefore as you spiritualize your thoughts and feed your subconscious with life-giving patterns of wholeness, beauty, and perfection, the subconscious mind has no alternative but to be cleansed, and the healing will follow.

It is no use to petition God and beg and beseech that you may be healed. God does not respond to your petition, to your begging or beseeching or supplication. The God presence responds to your belief, to your conviction, to your understanding. According to your belief is it done unto you.

Permanent healing follows a real change of mind and heart, a reconditioning of your mind and heart. Announce the Kingdom of Heaven to your own mind. Teach your faculties—your disciples—to give up fear, hate, resentment, and false beliefs.

Teach your faculties not to judge according to appearances, that external thing are a condition. You don't give power to conditions. You give power to the spirit within you, and you allow the healing power to flow through you. Your disciples are your disciplined qualities of mind.

For example, you must discipline your vision. Where there is no vision, the people perish. If you envision yourself successful, whole, envision the doctor congratulating you on your perfect health and harmony, you'll go where your vision is. If you have a poor vision or a poor estimate or blueprint of yourself, you'll be sick, frustrated, neurotic.

When you have regularly, systemically, and vigorously reiterated to your mind the kingdom of harmony, health, and peace, and wisdom and beauty and boundless love are all within you, lodged in your deeper mind; when you convince yourself that the infinite healing presence which made you is Almighty, that there's nothing to oppose it or challenge it, that it is there waiting to be released, then your vision will soar, your faith will be kindled, and wonders will happen in your life. Healing will follow, for all things be ready if the mind be so.

Know that there's one presence and one power, and none else. Know this, and you will give power to nothing else in the universe.

There is no principle of disease. There is nothing to sustain it. It's a product of destructive thinking. Therefore, as you change your thought to conform to universal principles, your body must change. This is the law of mind.

Remember, the body is characterized by inertia. Quimby brought this out over 100 years ago. He said, "Your body moves as moved upon. Your body acts as acted upon." In other words, you can play on your body a melody of love or a hymn of hate. Your body doesn't care.

Your body is a confluence of atoms. It's molecular. Thus your body is characterized by inertia—remember that. It cannot originate any movement. There's no initiative, no self-conscious intelligence, no volition in and of itself, no more so than a stone. You have to move a stone from one place to another, don't you?

Your body is composed of primordial substance. It is molded by your thought. Change your thinking to conform to spiritual standards, and you will have new cells and new tissues as you fill your mind with eternal verities and the truths of God.

Suppose you sever your arm or your leg from the body and you put it on a shelf or on a table. It cannot get cancer, tuberculosis, ringworm, or any disease under the sun. Why? Because it's separated from the mind. It will undergo disintegration, which is a natural phenomenon, but that's not disease.

For example, supposing your thoughts are full of fear and anxiety and worry. You may well get gastritis, which is an inflammation of the lining of your stomach. You may get ulcers. Modern psychosomatic physicians tell us that negative emotions are behind ulcers and all diseases.

Suppose you have the ulcers excised by a surgeon, and you continue to worry and fret and fume and be full of hostility and so on. Even though you continue with your bland diet, you'll get ulcers again. Surgery isn't really the answer.

Thousands and thousands of people have been healed of ulcers by filling their mind with the truths of God, establishing peace and harmony, thinking on whatsoever things are true, whatsoever things are just, whatsoever things are lovely, whatsoever things are pure, and whatsoever things are honest. Thinking from the standpoint of harmony, health, peace, and love and goodwill, filling their mind with these eternal truths. Then they have a new body, because you have a new body every eleven months, with new cells, tissues, bones, and everything.

There is no such thing as an incurable disease. There are incurable people who believe they can't be healed. Many people have been healed of malignancies. They have broken the shell while others haven't, because of the intensity of the fear buried in their subconscious mind.

• • •

The consciousness of love is the greatest healing power there is. There are many people who are untutored, unlettered, who have no knowledge of anatomy or physiology, but they have a great consciousness of love. They're marvelous healers. Doctors and surgeons and others are amazed at the miraculous healing performed by these unlettered people.

It is a consciousness of love that contemplates the wonders of it all, an infinite intelligence that guides the planets on their course, that causes the sun to shine. They realize also that here is an infinite intelligence which enables the astronomers to tell us when Halley's Comet will return to a split second, and governs the entire cosmos with undeviating laws and principles.

They realize the indescribable beauty of God, they realize absolute harmony in nature, they realize the divine love and plant it in all of us. We see it in the mother who goes all over the world trying to heal her child suffering from infantile paralysis or spasms, or the brother who serves time for his sister and says he committed the crime, or the soldier in battle who says, "Well, I'm not married, I have no children." He gives his life for his comrades.

Yet all of that love, however wonderful it is, is but a faint shadow of that infinite ocean of God's love. Therefore the people with that consciousness of love, realizing that the will of God for all men is life, love, truth, and beauty, who build that consciousness of love within them, they are the greatest healers.

Dr. Flanders Dunbar, who earned degrees in theology and is a distinguished psychiatrist as well as a medical doctor, has written a book called *Emotions and Bodily Diseases,* and in it brought out an interesting case.

She spoke about a Dr. Groddich, who reported that a shoemaker was going blind. The shoemaker attributed it to, of course, his work. He was told to give it up, but however, his eyes didn't get any better. He suffered from retinal hemorrhages. That is hemorrhages in the tiny blood vessels of his eyes.

Now, what did the doctor do? He said it was psychogenic. Psychogenic simply means "of emotional origin." He went to work on this man and discovered the things he didn't want to see in life, the things he resented, and so forth. He got him to give up his negative condition, his negative emotions, and his eyes were restored.

Psychosomatic authorities, meaning doctors who study the psyche of the soul of man and emotions, report that glaucoma and a detached retina are associated with mental and emotional disturbances.

I read a few years ago that there were 500 cases of glaucoma admitted to the Chicago Eye and Ear and Throat Hospital in Chicago. Research workers discovered that about 25% of them had hatred toward relatives, which affects the eyes.

Something you don't want to see, what you want to shut out in your world. What do you wish to exclude? Your subconscious mind goes to work on that because that's your command to your subconscious, and it brings about an occlusion of your vision.

Dr. Dunbar recites a case where a woman was taken to a mental asylum, and her sister began to lose her sight. Why? Because she felt guilty that she hadn't been kind to her sister. She wanted to punish herself. She said, "I didn't treat her right. I'm guilty," and so on.

When the doctors went to work on her and told her, after all, it wasn't her fault that her sister was carried to a psychiatric ward, and that was the cause of her retinal condition, she was restored to inward peace through psychological and psychotherapeutic treatment. Her eyes cleared up perfectly.

She realized what she was doing to herself, and of course, that she had to forgive herself as well as her sister, to bless her sister and stop condemning herself. Self-condemnation knows the curse of curses. Self-condemnation and self-criticism are highly destructive.

Some years ago, a doctor friend of mine, a surgeon, had ulcers in his right hand. We got talking one day, and he said, "You know this hand of mind doesn't heal, and I can't operate. I've tried everything under the sun. I've gone to specialists, I've tried ointments and lotions, I've tried x-ray therapy, all manner of therapy, and yet these ulcers continue."

I said to him, "Doctor, why do you think it's the right hand? The right is your objective world in the

Bible, and the left is the subjective. Did you do something for which you feel guilty?"

He said, "Yes," and he blushed. "But that was years ago when I was an intern."

I said, "Would you do it now?"

He said, "No. I would not."

"You're condemning an innocent man," I told him. "You're not the same man. Mentally, you're not the same. You have a new vision of life. Emotionally, you're not the same, nor physiologically or physically, because every 11 months we have a new body, including our bones. And spiritually, you're certainly not the same man.

"You're condemning an innocent man, and no one is condemning you. The God presence doesn't condemn. If you cut yourself, it heals you. If you burn yourself, it reduces the edema, gives you new skin and tissue. The tendency of life is to heal the will of God, for everyone is life, love, truth, and beauty, transcending your fondest dreams.

"The tendency of life is to heal, to restore. Even the psychotic, the raving maniac, the tendency of life is to restore that person to harmony, health, and peace. That's the movement of life. That's the rhythm of life. That's the way of life, and God is the life principle animating all men, and the God presence can't be sick and frustrated so its tendency is to heal, to express itself through you as rhythm, order, beauty, and proportion.

"You are condemning yourself, and as long as you're condemning yourself, you can't be healed. You can't hold onto your blindness and expect a healing. You can't hold onto self-condemnation, self-criticism, which are blocking the healing. It's just the same as if in your sink, the pipe is stopped up with debris and corrosion and rust. The water is waiting to come through, but it can't."

My explanation was the cure. In a week's time, the ulcers healed and he was able to operate again, and he was able to play a musical instrument that he loved to play.

Yet for two years his hand was not healed because of self-condemnation, self-criticism, and guilt. With that feeling of guilt comes the idea that one must be punished. With that, of course, comes fear.

All of this is false belief. No being in the sky is punishing you, man punishes himself. God can't punish anyone. The absolute can't punish. All judgment is given to the sun, the sun is your mind, and according to your own thoughts and feelings it's done unto you.

Dr. Flanders Dunbar says that the skin, more than any other part of the body, shows the relationship of man's thought and feeling, of his emotions to his health. She brings out the great truth that the skin is the place where the inner world communicates with the external world, and that skin conditions are usually due to hostility, repressed emotions, anger, rage, self-condemnation, self-criticism, or emotional protest against something in the inner life.

These are very interesting things to realize, for the Bible knew that thousands of years ago. The men who wrote the Bible said, "As a man thinketh in his heart, so is he." The heart is your subconscious mind. It's the seat of emotions, the seat of feeling.

Thinking in the heart, there are many buried thoughts and beliefs in your mind that have a life of their own, and these subconscious assumptions and beliefs dictate and control all of your conscious actions.

One man believes that his condition is incurable. He says his mother had cancer, his father died of cancer, and so forth. Others say that's nonsense, that cancer is the product of destructive thinking, conscious and unconscious. If one changes their thinking, they'll change their body.

I told you about the Episcopal priest a few years ago. It was written up in a New York paper how he had cancer. His surgeon told him it was metastasizing in his system. He got members of his congregation to pray and began to pray himself. He went back to the surgeon after a while, suffering excruciating pain, and received x-ray therapy. The surgeon told him it was breaking up, that he was going to be well.

He was completely healed, and the newspaper article said, "It's now five years later. That man is perfectly whole." He believed there was an Almighty power, which meant his body could heal him, and he was restored.

There are a lot of people who break that shell, because as you change your mind, you change your body. Your body can't get sick. No sickness is independent of the mind, as I've explained.

Spiritual healing is a very real thing. It is the miraculous healing power within you that made you. Therefore, as you turn to it and realize it is now really seeing itself as whole, as beauty and perfection, and as you fill your mind with these truths of God, and as you forgive everybody including yourself, then of course you'll have a marvelous healing.

If we are blind and adhere to our blindness, then of course we can't be healed. Blindness is man's ignorance, his superstition, and his fear, his belief that the will of God gave him his suffering. That's blindness.

Realize that it's normal and natural for you to be healthy, happy, joyous, and free, and realize your body is an instrument in which God dwells. You're the tabernacle of the living God.

You can't be free of your illnesses and cling to ill will, bitterness, self-condemnation, hate, resentment. The alcoholic can't be healed and still adhere to his self-condemnation, self-criticism, his sense of guilt, and his hatred, his loathing of himself. He must give up all of these. He must have goodwill in his heart for everyone, for love is the fulfilling of the law of health and harmony.

He must pull from it love, peace, and goodwill and wish for every living being in the world what he wishes for himself. He will know when he is forgiven because he can meet the person in his mind, and there's no sting, but a wave of peace and goodwill.

The healing presence is within you, and wonders can happen in your life as you begin to turn to it. *"Great peace have they who love thy law,"* and wonders happen in their life. Those who have found that inner peace—great peace have they who love thy law—nothing shall offend them.

"With mine eyes stayed on thee, there is no evil in my pathway." The divine presence is everlasting within you. Realize now that the miraculous healing powers focused at that point in your mind where the problem is causes it to shatter, making way for the healing power of God to flow through you.

You do not create vision, for example, but rather you manifest or release it. We see *through* the eye, not with it. The cornea of the eye is stimulated by light waves from objects in space through the optic nerve, and these stimuli are carried to the brain. When the inner light or intelligence meet the outer light in this manner, by a process of interpretation, we see. Your eyes symbolize divine love and delight in the ways of God, plus a hunger and thirst for God's truth.

Your right eye symbolizes right thought and right action. The left eye symbolizes God's love and wisdom. Think right and radiate goodwill to all, and you will focus perfectly. *"Receive thy sight,"* He said, *"and immediately he received his sight, and following him, glorified God."*

Millions of people are blind. That is, they're psychologically and spiritually blind because they do not know that they become what they think all day long. Man is spiritually and mentally blind when he's hateful, resentful, or envious of others. He does not know that he's actually secreting mental poisons which tend to destroy him. That's his sickness, that's his disease. Disease is a lack of peace, a lack of equilibrium. All sickness is due to ill will.

Thousands of people are constantly saying that there is no way to solve their problems and their situation is hopeless. They're saying, "God can't heal me." Yet at the same time they're saying, "With God, all things are possible." They say, "From whom all blessings flow." But you see, they're atheists. They're denying what they're affirming.

Such an attitude is the result of spiritual blindness. Man begins to see spiritually and mentally when he gets a new understanding of his mental powers and develops a conscious awareness that the wisdom and intelligence in his subconscious can solve all his problems. Everyone should become aware of the inter-relationship and interaction of the conscious and subconscious mind.

Persons who were once blind to these truths, after careful introspection, will now begin to see the vision of health, wealth, happiness, and peace of mind that can be theirs through the correct application of the laws of mind and the way of the spirit.

Yes, the healing power of God is within you, and wonders can happen in your life as you begin to say *God in the midst of me is healing me now*. No mental or religious science practitioner, psychologist, psychiatrist, or medical doctor ever healed a patient. The psychologist or psychiatrist remove the mental blocks. Likewise, the surgeon removes the physical block, enabling the healing currents of God to flow through you.

There are many different methods used to remove the mental and emotional and physical blocks, which inhibit the flow of the healing life principle animating all of us. The healing principle resident in your subconscious mind can and will, if properly directed by you or someone else, heal your mind and body of all disease.

There is only one process of healing. There is only one universal healing principle operating through everything, for everything is alive, and God is life. This life principle operates through the animal, vegetable, and mineral kingdom as instinct and as law of growth.

•   •   •

There are many approaches, techniques, and methods using the universal power, but there is only one process of healing. That is faith, and according to your faith is it done unto you. All religions of the world represent forms of belief, and these beliefs are explained in many ways. The law of life is the law of belief. What you believe about yourself, life, and the universe is done unto you as you believe.

Belief is a thought in your mind which causes the power of your subconscious to be distributed in all phases of your life. Whether the object of your belief be true or false, you will get the same results. It's far better to know what you're doing and why you're doing it. Then, it is scientific prayer.

You must realize the Bible is not talking about your belief in some ritual, ceremony, form, institution, man, or formula. It is talking about belief in itself. The belief of your mind is simply the thought of your mind. *"If thou canst believe, all things are possible to him that believeth."*

Spiritual treatment or therapy means that you turn to the indwelling God and remind yourself of God's peace, harmony, wholeness, beauty, boundless love, and limitless power. Know that God loves you and cares for you. As you pray this way, the fear will gradually fade. If you pray about a heart condition, do not think of the organ as diseased, as this would not be spiritual thinking.

Thoughts are things. Your spiritual thought takes the form of cells, tissues, nerves, and organs. To think of a damaged heart or high blood pressure tends to suggest more of what you already have. Cease dwelling on symptoms, organs, or any part of the body. Turn your mind to God and his love. Feel and know that there's only one healing presence and power, and to its corollary, there is no power to challenge the action of God.

Quietly and lovingly affirm that the uplifting, healing, strengthening power of the infinite healing presence is flowing through you, making you whole. Know and feel that the harmony, beauty, and love of God manifests itself in you as strength, peace, vitality, wholeness, and right action.

Get a clear realization of this, and the damaged heart or other diseased organ will be cured in the light of God's love. God in the midst of you is healing you now. Glorify God in your body now and forever more.

Pray and Prosper

To prosper means to succeed, to thrive, to turn out well. It means to grow spiritually, mentally, financially, and intellectually, in all ways. In other words, when you're prospering, you're expanding, growing financially, socially, intellectually, and of course spiritually.

In order to truly prosper, it is necessary that you become a channel through which the life principle flows freely, harmoniously, joyously, and lovingly. I suggest that you establish a definite method of working and thinking and that you practice it regularly and systematically every day.

One young man who consulted with me had experienced a poverty complex for many years, and had received no answers to his prayers. He had prayed for prosperity, but the fear of poverty continuously weighed on his mind. Naturally, he attracted more lack and limitation. The subconscious mind accepts the dominant of two ideas.

After talking with me, he began to realize that his thought image of wealth produces wealth, and that every thought is creative unless it is neutralized by a counter thought of greater intensity. Furthermore, he realized that his thought and belief about poverty was greater than his belief in the infinite riches all around him. Consequently, he changed his thoughts and kept them changed.

I rolled out a prosperity prayer for him as follows. You can use it.

I know there's only one source, the life principle from which all things flow. The whole world was here when you were born. Who created you? You came out of the invisible yourself. That life principle is working in you growing hair on your face, on your head, and growing your nails, watching over you when you're sound asleep. It created the universe and all things therein contained. Then, you say to yourself:

"I'm a focal point of the divine presence. My mind is open and receptive. I am a free-flowing channel for harmony, beauty, guidance, wealth, and the riches of the infinite. I know that health, wealth, and success are released from within and appear on the without. I am now in harmony with the infinite riches within and without, and I know these thoughts are sinking into my subconscious mind. Like seeds, they grow after their kind.

"They will be reflected on the screen of space. I wish for everyone all the blessings of life. I am openly receptive to the infinite riches, spiritual, mental, and material, and they flow to me in ava-lanches of abundance."

This young man focused his thoughts on God's riches rather than on poverty, and made it a special point not to deny what he affirmed. In a month's time his whole life was transformed. He affirmed the above truths morning and evening for about 10 minutes, slowly and quietly, realizing that by osmosis they sink from the conscious into the subconscious mind. Ideas are conveyed to the subconscious by repetition, faith, and expectancy.

Knowing that he was actually writing down these truths in his subconscious mind gave him faith, caus-ing the subconscious mind to be activated and to release his hidden treasures. Although he had been a salesman for 10 years with rather dim prospects for the future, he was made sales manager at $30,000 a year plus prime benefits.

You can prosper. The thought image of wealth pro-duces wealth. You can begin to use it now, and there is a marvelous power within you that will respond. The whole world and all its treasures in the sea, air, and earth were here when you were born.

Begin to think of the untold and undiscovered riches all around you, waiting for the intelligence of man to bring them forth. For example, oil was in the ground long before any man walked this earth. So was coal, copper, and nickel. It took a guiding principle within man to discover the treasures in the earth, in the air, and in the sea.

A sales manager said to me the other day that an associate of his sold a million-dollar idea for expansion to the organization for which he worked. He also added that there were more millionaires now in the United States than at any time in history.

You can have an idea worth a fortune, however you are here to release the imprisoned splendor within you and surround yourself with the luxury, beauty, and the riches of life.

The Chinese have an old saying: "Make friends with money, and you'll always have it." That's true. You can learn that it is necessary to have the right attitude toward money. When you really make friends with money, you will always have a surplus.

Prosperity means that you have all the money you need to do what you want to do when you want to do it. Then you're as rich as Croesus. If you want to take your wife to Europe, you can do it. If you want to buy her a fur coat just because the weather is cold in the evening, you should have the money to go out and buy it.

It should be circulating in your life, and there should always be a surplus. Then you would be economically healthy. You would be prosperous. You would be successful, too.

It is normal and natural for you to desire a fuller, richer, happier, and more wonderful life. If you don't, you're abnormal. Look upon money as God's idea of maintaining the economic health of the nations of the world. When money is circulating freely in your life, you are economically healthy. In the same manner as when your blood is circulating freely, you are free from congestion.

Begin now to see money in its true significance and role in life as a symbol of exchange. Money to you should mean freedom from want. It should mean beauty, luxury, abundance, a sense of security, and refinement.

Being poor is a mental attitude. Poverty is a disease of the mind. You can never eradicate the slums in the world, nor eradicate the slums in the mind of man.

If you have any hang-ups, get that hang-up. There's nothing good or bad, but thinking makes it so. God pronounced the world good and his creation good and very good.

All evil comes from misinterpretation of life and misuse of the laws of the mind. You can use electricity to fry an egg or vacuum the floor, or to electrocute a man. You can use atomic energy to sail a ship across the ocean, or you can use it to kill a quarter of a million Japanese when the war was over.

In other words, the only evil is ignorance, and the only consequence is suffering. It would be foolish, insipid, and silly to pronounce uranium, silver, lead, copper, iron, cobalt, nickel, calcium, or a dollar bill evil. The only difference between one metal and another is the number and rate of motions of electrons revolving around the central nucleus. A piece of paper such as a hundred dollar bill is innocuous, and the only difference between it and copper or lead is that the atoms and molecules with their electrons and protons are arranged differently.

. . .

Love in biblical language is to give your allegiance, loyalty, and faith to the source of all things, which is, of course, the God presence, the life principle within you. Therefore you are not to give your allegiance, loyalty, and trust to created things, but to the Creator, the source of everything in the universe, from the apple on the tree to the air you breathe to the water you drink.

If a man says, "All I want is money and nothing else, that's my God, and nothing but money matters," he can get it, of course, but he is here to lead a balanced life. Man must also claim peace, harmony, beauty, guidance, love, joy, and wholeness in all phases of his life.

To make money the sole aim in life would constitute an error or wrong choice. You must express your hidden talents. You'll find your true place in life. You must experience the joy of contributing to the growth, happiness, and success of others in your family.

As you apply the laws of your subconscious in the right way, you can have all the money you want and still have peace of mind, harmony, wholeness, and serenity. To accumulate money to the exclusion of everything else causes man to become lopsided and unbalanced. All the Bible means is that you look to the source, honor the source, and that source never runs dry. But you can't depend upon externals for peace, health, happiness, joy, abundance, or anything else.

The oil well can dry up, banks close down, and governments change. All these things happen, but there is that within you that never changes. It's the eternal source, and as you unite with that and say God's wealth is circulating in my life, that there's always a surplus, you'll never want for any good thing.

No matter what form money takes, you'll always have it, and you'll have plenty of it. You don't want enough to go around—that's stupid. You want plenty to spare. You want abundance. You want it circulating in your life. Think of all the good things you can do for yourself and your family.

There is a tremendous source within you. As I told you, it's inexhaustible. I have taught this in many parts of the world. Take a couple of words. *Success.* *Wealth.* Whether you admit there's wealth, don't you walk down the street? That's all you see is wealth, and you admit that the infinite can fail.

So, there are two words, and just before you go to sleep, take these two words, *success, wealth, success, wealth.* Repeat it slowly over and over again, silently or audibly, and fall asleep with these two words on your lips.

What will happen? They'll sink into your subconscious mind, and the subconscious will compel you to express wealth and success, because the nature of the subconscious is compulsion. Therefore by repeating these ideas, they sink down into your subconscious mind, and like seeds, they come forth after their time.

There is a young boy, Robbie Wright, who operates my tape machine. He recently was afraid to go into calculus. I said, "Do the thing you're afraid to do. The professor couldn't ask you except he believed in you. The infinite within you can't fail. It will give you all the ideas you need."

He has taken it up, and he's going ahead by leaps and bounds, and has been made president of his class.

That's wealth, too, you know. It means to prosper, to grow every way. Because you don't want to be a mediocre doctor do you? You want to be a great doctor. You want to be outstanding, you want to be able to heal people, and you don't want to be mediocre.

The Cure for
Hurt Feelings

Some months ago, I had a letter from a man who stated that he couldn't understand why everybody around him annoyed him. I asked him to come see me, and in talking with him, I discovered that he was constantly rubbing others the wrong way.

He did not like himself and was full of self-condemnation. He spoke in a very tense, irritable tone. His asperity of speech grated on one's nerves. He thought meanly of himself and was highly critical of others.

I explained to him that while his unhappy experiences seemed to be with other people, his relationship with them was determined by his thoughts and feelings about himself and them. I elaborated on the fact that if he despises himself, he cannot have goodwill and respect for others. It's impossible because it is a law of mind that he is always projecting his thoughts and feelings onto his associates and all those around him. That's called projection.

He began to realize that as long as he projected feelings of prejudice, ill will, and contempt for others, that is exactly what he would get back because his world is but an echo of his moods and attitudes.

I gave him a mental and spiritual formula that enabled him to overcome his irritation and arrogance. He decided to write consciously the following thoughts in his subconscious mind. Remember your conscious mind is a pen, and you can write anything you want in your subconscious mind. This is what he wrote:

"I'll practice the Golden Rule from now on. I mean it. This means that I think, speak, and act toward others as I wish others to think, speak, and act toward me. I walk serenely on my way, and I am free, for I give freedom to all. I sincerely wish peace, prosperity, and success to all. I'm always poised, serene, and calm. The peace of the infinite floods my mind and my whole being. Others appreciate and respect me as I appreciate myself. Life is honoring me greatly, for it has provided for me abundantly. The petty things of life no long irritate or annoy me.

"When fear, worry, doubt, or criticism by others come to me, and they knock at my door, faith and goodness, truth and beauty open the door in my mind. There's no one there. The suggestions and statements of others have no power. I know

now how to cure hurt feelings. The only power is in my own thought.

"When I think God's thoughts, God's power is with my thoughts of good. I know the thoughts of others have no power except the power that I give them. They have to become my thoughts; then it becomes a movement of my own thought."

He affirmed these truths morning, noon, and night, and committed the whole prayer to memory. He poured into these words life, love, and meaning, and by osmosis, these ideas penetrated the layers of his subconscious mind. He became a changed man.

He said to me, "I'm learning how to specialize myself out of the law of averages. I'm getting along fine. I've received two promotions in the past two months. I now know the truth of the passage, *'If I be lifted up, I will draw men, all manifestation, unto me.'*" Lift it up in your mind.

He learned the trouble was within himself. He decided to change his thoughts, feelings, and reactions. Any man can do the same. It takes decisions, stick-to-itiveness, and a keen desire to transform oneself.

•   •   •

Ralph Waldo Emerson said, "There is one mind common to all individual men. Every man is an inlet to the same and to all of the same." He also said, "He who has admitted to the right of reason is a freeman of the whole estate."

Begin to realize this. Realize that infinite intelligence, the guiding principle of the universe, is within you. The infinite healing presence controls all your vital organs and all the processes and functions of your body. You have the capacity to make choices, to use your imagination and all the other powers of God within you. Your mind is actually God's mind. When you consciously, decisively, and constructively use the infinite power within, you become a freeman of the whole estate.

Emerson inspired us to enlarge the concept of ourselves when he announced this profound truth. "What Plato has thought, man may think. What a saint has felt, he may feel. What at any time has fallen any man, he can understand. Who had access to the universe and mind is a party to all that is or can be done, for this is the only and sovereign agent."

Emerson was America's greatest philosopher and one of the greatest thinkers of all time. He was constantly in tune with the infinite. He urged all men to release the infinite possibilities within them. Emerson taught the dignity and grandeur of man and pointed out to his listeners that the great appear great to us because we are on our knees, that we attribute greatness to Plato and others because they acted upon what they themselves thought and not upon what other people believed, of what others thought they should think.

Begin to have a lofty, noble, and dignified concept of yourself, and the petty things of life will no longer irritate you. If they do, you're emotionally immature. You're suffering from infantilism. That's why people say, "Why don't you act your age? Why don't you grow up?"

Are your feathers easily ruffled when someone in your department says, "Get on the ball. You're behind the eight ball," or do you take it in stride and say, "Well, he's right. I'm going to have a better showing the next time."

Remember what the psalm has said to all men: *"I have said you are gods, and all of you are children of the most high."* And you are. Everyone is a child of the most high. The infinite is within you. There's a right way to talk, to walk, to drive a car, to bake a cake. There's a right and wrong way to do everything.

To live a full and happy life, you must live according to principles. You would not think of building a wheel off-center or violating the principle of electricity or chemistry. Likewise, when you think, speak, act, and react from the standpoint of the infinite intelligence within you, you will find that your whole life will be one of happiness, success, and peace of mind.

• • •

Mrs. Wrongway was jealous and hateful toward a supervisor in her office, suffering from hurt feelings. She had developed ulcers and high blood pressure. However when she became interested in the spiritual principle of forgiveness and goodwill, she realized that she had accumulated many resentful and grudging attitudes and that these negative and obnoxious thoughts were festering in her subconscious mind.

She tried to talk with her supervisor in an effort to straighten matters out, but the woman brushed her off. In a continuing effort to correct this situation, Mrs. Wrongway applied the principles of harmony and goodwill for ten minutes every morning and night, prior to going to work. This is what she did. She affirmed as follows: "I surround Mrs. X with harmony, love, peace, joy, and goodwill."

Now this is not mumbo-jumbo. She knew what she was doing and why she was doing it. These thoughts or ideas sink into the subconscious. There's only one subconscious mind, and the other person picks it up. She said, "There are harmony, peace, and understanding between us, and whenever I think of Mrs. X, I will say, 'God's love saturates your mind.'"

A few weeks passed, and Mrs. Wrongway went to San Francisco for a weekend. Boarding the plane, she discovered that the only vacant seat was the one next to her supervisor. She greeted her cordially and received a cordial and loving response. They had a harmonious and joyous time together in San Francisco. They are now attending these lectures on Sunday morning at the Wilshire Ebell Theatre.

Infinite intelligence set the stage for the solution of this difficulty in ways that Mrs. Wrongway didn't know, for the ways of your subconscious are past finding out. As the heavens are above the earth, so are its ways above you always.

Mrs. Wrongway's changed thinking had changed everything, including a perfect healing of her ulcers and high blood pressure. She was hurting herself. The other person is not responsible for the way you think or feel. Only you are, because you are the only thinker in your universe, and you are responsible for the way you think about your congressman, your senator, or anybody else. The other fellow is not.

I recall a young woman saying to me one time, "Everybody in my office dislikes me. There are several who want me fired."

I said to her, "Why don't you resign and find another position?"

She said, "What's the use? I've had six jobs this year so far." This young lady had a brilliant mind, was well educated, and was an outstanding legal secretary. Ninety percent of her problems were in her personality.

Did you know that over ninety percent of all the problems in the factory and the school, in business and government, in the home are not technical? They're man's and woman's inability to get along with others. They're rubbing others the wrong way. Personality conflicts, personality troubles. Over ninety percent of her problem was in her personality, but the tendency is to blame others.

I gave her a spiritual prescription and suggested that she take it regularly, morning and night, for several months. I told her to pray the following prayer for every man and woman in her office every day before she went to work:

"I send out loving thoughts and feelings of goodwill, happiness, and joy to all those in my office. I affirm, claim, and believe that my relationship with each one of my coworkers will be harmonious, pleasant, and satisfactory. Divine love, harmony, peace, and beauty flow through my thoughts, words, and deeds, and I am constantly releasing the imprisoned splendor within me. I am happy, joyous, and free, bubbling over with enthusiasm, and I rejoice in the goodness of God in the land of the living and in the innate goodness of all people."

This is something she had reiterated and remained faithful to, and when thoughts of anger, criticism, or being hurt came to her, she would pour forth goodwill upon others. At the end of two months, she received a wonderful promotion and was put in charge of the entire legal office.

For example, a thought comes to you, that you'd like to wring somebody's neck. What's to prevent you from saying God's peace filled your soul? Not a thing in the world.

The law of substitution takes a little practice. Anyone can do it who wants to do it. How much do you want what you want? Do you want to give up your grudges, your hurt feelings, your resentment, antagonism, and get good digestion and a normal blood pressure? You have to give up something.

A man whom I was interviewing recently said to me, "I'm all mixed up and tied up. I can't get along with others. I'm constantly rubbing them the wrong way." This young man was hypersensitive, jittery, self-centered, and crotchety. In spite of all this, he wanted to have good relations with his co-workers and to get along with them in every respect.

I explained to him that his present personality represented the sum total of his habitual thinking, training, indoctrination, and emotional atmosphere, plus the sum total of beliefs inculcated upon his mind, but that he could transform himself.

I explained to him that the infinite indwelled him, that all the attributes, potencies, qualities, and aspects of the infinite were lodged in his deeper mind and could be resurrected and expressed in his personal life. You're transformed by renewal of your mind, you know. I gave him the following prayer for the purposes of transforming his entire personality. He affirmed feelingly and lovingly several times a day:

"God is a great personality, the one life being expressed through me. God is the infinite life principle within me, and this presence flows through me now as harmony, joy, peace, love, beauty, and power. I am a channel for the divine in the same way that a bulb is a channel for electricity. The wholeness, beauty, and perfection of the infinite are constantly being expressed through me.

"Today I am reborn spiritually. I completely detach myself from my old way of thinking. I bring divine life, love, truth, and beauty into my experience. I consciously feel love for everyone. I radiate it. I exude it. Mentally, I say to everyone I contact, 'I see the divine presence in you. I know you see the divine presence in me.'

"I recognize the qualities of the infinite in everyone. I practice this morning, noon, and night. It is a living part of me. I am reborn spiritually now because all day long, I practice the presence of the infinite. No matter what I am doing, whether I'm walking along the street, shopping, or going about my daily business, whenever my thought wanders away from the infinite, I bring it back to the contemplation of the divine holy presence. I feel noble, dignified, and godlike. I walk in a high mood, sensing my oneness with the infinite. His peace fills my soul."

Has this man made a habit of allowing attributes and qualities of the infinite good to flow through his mind? His whole personality underwent a marvelous change because a personality is the sum total of your thinking, your feeling, your beliefs, and your conditioning.

He became affable, amiable, urbane, and more understanding. He now communicates vibrancy and goodwill wherever he goes. In addition, he's moved up several rungs on the ladder of success in the field of work. *"Great peace have they who love thy law, and nothing shall offend them."* Always I am that which I contemplate. I am that which I feel myself to be.

"Thou wilt keep Him in perfect peace whose mind is stayed on thee because he trusteth in thee." With your eyes stayed on God, there is no evil on your pathway. Divine love goes before you today and every day, making stray joyous and glorious happy your way.

A husband and wife were quarreling recently. Both were suffering from hurt pride, their egos were deflated. The wife was weeping, had the crying jags, temper tantrums. Both were very angry, glowering at each other. Both accusing each other, blaming each other. They had a six-year-old daughter, and she looked at both of them and said, "Both of you deserve a good spanking!" The husband and wife laughed, the tension was broken. They had to laugh at themselves, as they were silly, the whole episode ludicrous and irrational. They were enjoying hurt feelings.

Psychic trauma robs you of vitality, wholeness, beauty, and energy. You can't afford hurt feelings because they're robbing you of everything worthwhile—it's the quickest way in the world to get old, wrinkled, and sick. It's very expensive medicine. It robs you of everything worthwhile.

There are some people who get a morbid, pseudo-satisfaction out of playing the martyr role. They say, "If you loved me, you would do thus and so." Some say, "Oh, I will be dead and gone, and you'll be sorry for the way you treated me. You're giving me a heart attack. You're killing me now."

This is emotional blackmail. They are trying to get you to do what they want you to do. They're certainly not interested in your welfare, but they're selfish, they're possessive. They say, "Do what I want you to do," yet are not the slightest bit interested in your happiness, your peace, your joy.

Do you want all your relatives and associates to think the way you do, to believe the way you do, to act the way you wish them to act, to vote the same way, to go to the same church? If you do, you're emotionally immature. It's called infantilism. You haven't grown up.

Give your relatives, your grandfather, your grandmother, everybody, give them their freedom. Permit them to believe what they want to believe. If they want to believe in a devil, permit them to believe in it. Let them have their peculiarities, abnormalities, eccentricities, and unconventional ways.

There's a wonderful saying, MYOB, which means "mind your own business." People in your life have the right to do what they think is right, and you have the right to do what you think is right. You're here to do right, think right, act right, and be right. You're here to be a producer. You're here to contribute to the world.

What do you produce? Harmony, health, peace, joy, abundance, security. You have no time for criticism, condemnation, self-pity, or criticism of others because you're too busy with your own work. You're bringing forth great things. Your success, prosperity, peace, and happiness are not dependent on what others think, what others do or don't do, what they say or don't say, what they think or don't think, what they believe or don't believe.

The only thing that matters is what you think in your heart, and your heart is your subconscious, meaning as you think and feel, so are you. You're responsible for the way you think. Your relatives aren't. You're responsible for your reactions, your thoughts, your feelings, your emotions. You're the master, you're the king.

The suggestions, statements, actions of others have no power to disturb you. You disturb yourself by the movement of your own thought. Therefore, you have the opportunity to curse or bless. If someone calls you a skunk, do you say, "Now, wait a minute, am I skunk? Do I smell like one?" You can say, "Sister, you can't disturb me today." God's peace fills your soul, and you go on about your business.

You refuse to give that person the power to give you a headache or disturb you emotionally, or cause you to be irrational and make a fool out of yourself, which is maybe what the other person wants. You're too smart for that.

"Jealousy is cruel as the grave," the Song of Solomon says. *"Its flashes are flashes of fire amidst vehement flame."* Jealous competition plays havoc with man. A jealous person is childish, and he looks that way. Did you ever look at a jealous person, man, or woman in business or profession or in the home life?

A jealous man in business is minding and interfering with the other fellow's business. His thought is on the other fellow, his actions when he comes home, the prices in the window, how he's conducting his business, and all that. He doesn't seem to have any time for his business, he's not attending to his own business. He's working for the other fellow all day long. He gets no pay for it. Isn't that a waste of energy and vitality and enthusiasm? It certainly is.

You please others best when you give the best you have of your talent, your ability, your time, and everything else. Do you think you're blocked by the person you're jealous of? No. Your thought governs you. Your belief governs you. You're a slave to the other person.

If there's a woman jealous of another, she feels inferior. She's full of fear. She has a rejection complex.

She's placing the other person on the pedestal and saying, "You're way up there, and I'm way down here." She's demoting herself and certainly attracting lack and limitation and impoverishing herself along all lines. It's disastrous.

Some time ago, I received a letter from a woman in Arizona. She said that her sister-in-law and mother-in-law disapproved of her, told her bluntly that they preferred her husband's former wife. They never invited her to their homes but always asked her husband to visit them alone.

Furthermore, although she tried her utmost to be nice to them, they criticized her meals, her home, her clothing, and her speech. This woman said that she felt inferior and rejected and asked me, "Why do they do this? What's wrong with me?"

In reply, I pointed out that she'd been suffering unnecessarily and without real warrant and that she had the power to refuse and to reject the poisonous statements of her in-laws, their rudeness and their incivility. I explained further that she did not create her mother-in-law or sister-in-law and that she was not responsible for their jealous, envious attitudes and complexes.

I told her to stop placing them on a pedestal and to stop being a doormat for them. A doormat is something one walks on, they wipe their feet on it. I added that it was quite possible that her charm, graciousness, kindness, and wonderful character annoyed them, and that they probably got a sadistic satisfaction in disturbing her.

I suggested that she break off all relations with them and cease abasing herself by kowtowing to them. I told her she needed an attitude of self-respect and self-esteem. I gave her the following prayer to be used three times a day, where it would sink into her subconscious mind:

"I completely surrender my in-laws to God. God made them and sustains them. I radiate love, peace, and goodwill to them. I wish for them all the blessings of life. I'm a child of the infinite. The infinite loves me and cares for me. He created me, sustains me.

"When a negative thought of anger, fear, self-criticism, self-condemnation, or resentment enters into my mind, I immediately supplant it with the thought of the infinite in the midst of me. I know I have complete dominion over my thoughts and emotions. I am the boss. I am the king over my conceptive realm.

"I am a channel of the divine, and I'll redirect all my feelings and emotions along harmonious, constructive lines. I refuse to give power to my in-laws to disturb me or any man, woman, or child.

Only God's ideas enter my mind, bringing me harmony, health, and peace. Whenever I'm drawn to demean or demote myself, I will boldly affirm I exalt God in the midst of me. I'm one with the infinite, and one with the infinite is a majority. If God be for me, who can be against me?"

She followed the above prayer and carried out the other instructions. You can do the same thing.

She said, "Thank you for the enclosed prayer. I phoned my in-laws and told them not to visit us at any time except when my husband and I issued a special invitation. I also told them that I sincerely wish them well, and I meant it. I see now where I made my mistake and how I was actually handicapping myself by thinking I was inferior to them. The prayer has worked wonders for me, and my husband said to me the other day, 'Honey, you're beaming. What happened to you?' I told him. Both of us are grateful."

That's the way to handle it. That's the way to cure hurt feelings, because you hurt yourself. Nobody has the power to hurt you. You hurt yourself as a movement of your own thought. Your thought is the king. Your thought is creative. As the other person's thought is relative, your thought is creative.

Does your belief about you and God govern you, or does the other person's belief govern you? Are you going to be hypnotized, mesmerized, brainwashed, manipulated by your mother-in-law or father-in-law, or don't you have a mind of your own? Don't you come to your own decisions? Isn't that an infinite intelligence within you, a guide, a counselor? Isn't there something within you that sustains and strengthens you? Surely, you don't take your instructions from your in-laws.

*   *   *

Some time ago, I had a consultation with a salesman. He said he was timid, shy, and resentful. He looked upon the world as harsh and cruel. Actually, he was trying to escape from taking his rightful dominion over life. He said his wife, his boss, and his associates didn't appreciate him. They criticized him. He was full of hurt feelings. His children looked down upon him.

The cause was that this young man had an inner sense of insecurity and inadequacy. He was down on himself. He said, "How can I gain the appreciation of others?"

I gave him a Biblical quotation: *Love thy neighbor as thyself.* The real meaning of this text is that your neighbor is yourself. The real self of you is the infinite intelligence within you. Speak thou to Him, for He hears in spirit, and spirit can meet closer, see them breathing near their hands and feet; another everyday meaning of the text to love your neighbor as you love yourself.

I explained to this young man the truth about himself and how to love and appreciate himself more along the following lines. If a man demotes, despises, and deprecates himself, he can't lift up or give esteem, goodwill, and respect to others, for it is a cosmic law of mind that man is constantly projecting his thoughts, feelings, and beliefs onto others, and what he sends out comes back to him.

If you're mean and cruel to yourself, others are going to be mean and cruel to you. The self of you is God as your higher self, as a supreme intelligence. Surely you should exalt that and honor it. That's love. That's your neighbor, and love means to be loyal and faithful, give your recognition, veneration to the supreme intelligence within you, and not to any created thing. Then you're loving God, which is your neighbor, the closest thing.

How could you love the fellow next door unless you first loved yourself? Man is the son of the infinite, and all the qualities and powers of the infinite are within him. Man must love and honor the indwelling presence. Love of self is to honor, recognize, exalt, respect, and give your allegiance to the living spirit within you, supreme and omnipotent.

The supreme intelligence made you, created you, animates and sustains you. It is the life principle within you. This has nothing to do with egoism or self-aggrandizement. On the contrary, it's a whole-some veneration for the divinity that shapes your ends.

The Bible says that your body is a temple of the infinite, that you're here to glorify the infinite. When you honor, respect, and love the self, you will auto-matically love, esteem, and honor others.

The salesman listened, and he said, "I've never heard it explained that way before. I can see clearly what I've been doing. I've been down on myself, and I've been full of prejudices, ill will, and bitterness. What I've been sending out has reverberated back to me. I've gained a true insight into myself."

This salesman practiced affirming the following truths with deep sincerity several times daily, know-ing they would sink down from his conscious to his subconscious mind, and like seeds, come forth after their kind:

"I know I can give only what I have. From this moment, I am going to have a wholesome, reverent, deep respect for my real self, which is the infinite. I'm an expression of the infinite, the infinite that needs me where I am, otherwise I would not be here. From this moment forward, I honor, respect, and salute the divinity in all my associates and all people everywhere. I hold the self of every person in veneration and esteem. I'm one with the infinite. I'm a tremendous success, and I wish for all men what I wish for myself, and I am at peace."

This transformed his life. He's no longer timid, shy, or resentful. He's gone ahead by leaps and bounds, and so can you. Learn to love your true self, and then you will learn to love and respect others.

"That thou seest, man, become too, thou must; God if thou seest God, dust if thou seest dust." Love the self of you, which is the "I am" within you. You say *I am* morning, noon, and night. When you say "I am," you're announcing the presence of the living God within you. It's called *Ehyeh*. It means being, life awareness, unconditioned, consciousness.

It's the self-originating spirit which Emerson spoke about. That's the spirit in you that created you. It's all-wise. It knows all and sees all. Surely, you should honor that. That's loving your neighbor as yourself.

The Great Law
of Security

"*When ye go, ye shall come unto a people secure and to a large land, for God hath given it into your hands, a place where there is no want to anything that is on the earth.*" This is from the Book of Judges.

You are secure when you walk in the realization that God indwells you, walks and talks in you. Realize you're always in the holy omnipresence surrounded by the sacred circle of God's eternal love. As you continue to do this, you will build up an immunity to all harm.

Claim, feel, and know that you and your family, your possessions, and all things appertaining to you are in the sacred place of the most high, watched over by an overshadowing presence which watches over you in all your ways. This is the impregnable fortress, invincible and impervious to everything negative.

In the above verse from Judges, it says, "*When ye go, ye shall come unto a people secure,*" meaning wherever you travel, divine love goes before you making stray joyous and happy your way. "*A place where there is no want"* means the presence of God is operating in your life, and *"the presence of God"* means a presence of harmony, peace, beauty, abundance, security.

Where there is the presence of God, there is no want. There is no sickness. There is no pain. Thou shalt be secure because there is hope. *"Yea, thou shall dig about thee, and thou shall take thy rest in safety."* That's from the Old Testament.

Hope springs eternal in the human breast. You may dig in the earth and find precious stones, jewels, oil, water, and other valuable things. When you dig within yourself, you discover the gold mine full of infinite riches within you. The precious stones are wisdom, truth, and beauty of inspiration; guidance, intuition, and creative ideas which heal, bless, elevate, and dignify your soul; ideas and the voice of intuition, which protects you, enabling you to sleep in peace every night and wake in joy because you live in God. Asleep, awake, or wherever you are, you realize divine love surrounds you, enfolds you, and enwraps you.

The first thing you have to realize is that there is no real security apart from your sense of oneness with God, the source of all blessings. By applying the principle of life, you can develop a practical, workable, sane, and marvelous feeling of inner security. There is an urge within each of us that cries out for union with an eternal source.

Join up now with that infinite presence and power, and you will immediately draw upon His strength. Because it is written, *"Call upon me; I will answer you. I'll be with you in trouble; I'll set you on high because you hath known my name."* The name is the nature of infinite intelligence, which is responsiveness. It responds to your thoughts.

You are immersed in the infinite ocean of life, the infinite presence and power, which constantly permeates you, entirely, and in which you live and move. Remember that this infinite presence and power has never been defeated or frustrated by anything outside itself. This infinite power is omnipotent, omniscient, and when you consciously unite with it, through your thought and feeling, you immediately become greater than that which you fear.

The infinite lies stretched in smiling repose within you. This is the true state of your mind. The power and wisdom of this infinite presence becomes potent and active in your life the moment you recognize its existence and establish your mental contact with it. If you do this now, you will experience immediately a marvelous feeling of inner security, and you will discover the peace that passeth all understanding.

•   •   •

A friend of mine was involved in a long-delayed lawsuit which had cost him a considerable sum of money in legal fees. His attorney had told him that he would probably lose the case, and this meant he would be more or less penniless. He was anxious, apprehensive, full of foreboding, and while discussing the matter said there was nothing left to live for and that the only thing to do was to end it all.

I explained to him that these utterances were highly destructive and undoubtedly played a major role in prolonging the case. Every time this man expressed these negative words, he had been praying against himself.

I asked him a simple question: "What would you say if I told you this minute that there had been a perfect, divine solution, where the whole matter was over with and settled harmoniously?"

He replied, "I would be delighted and eternally grateful. I would feel wonderful knowing that the whole thing was finished and done with." My friend then agreed to see to it that his inner silent thought would conform to his desired aim, which was a successful conclusion of the case. Regularly and systemically he applied the following prayer I gave him:

"I give thanks for the perfect, harmonious solution. I give thanks for the infinite justice, the

infinite harmony, and infinite right action operating in me, through me, and all around me, and
through everyone connected with this case."

He repeated this prayer to himself frequently
during the day, when difficulties, setbacks, delays,
false allegations and other things came to his mind.
He would silently affirm the great truth: There's a
divine, harmonious solution through the wisdom of
the Almighty. He completely ceased making negative
statements. He also controlled his silent thoughts,
knowing that his inner thought and feeling would
always be made manifest.

It is what you feel on the inside that is made manifest on the screen of space. You can say one thing with
your mouth and feel another way in your heart. It is
what you feel on the inside that is reproduced on the
screen of space.

This man learned through practice and discipline
never to affirm inwardly anything he did not want to
experience outwardly. His lips and his heart agreed on
a harmonious solution to his legal case, and divine justice prevailed. Additional information was provided
from a completely unexpected source, and the lawsuit
was resolved so that he did not suffer a financial loss.

My friend had realized that his security was dependent upon his alignment with the infinite presence,

within which moved as unity, harmony, justice, and right action. He discovered that nothing could oppose the infinite power that moves the world, because it is written, *"I hold before you an open door which no man can shut."* If you have not learned about your own essential greatness and the infinite power and presence within, you tend to magnify the problems and the difficulties which confront you, imparting to them powers in magnitude which you fail to attribute to yourself.

One of the main reasons for the feeling of insecurity is that you're making the externals of life causes, not realizing they're effects. The scientific thinker does not make the phenomenalistic world a cause. It's an effect, not a cause. You give power to the Creator, not the created thing.

Security cannot be legislated. No government, no matter how well-intentioned, can guarantee you peace, happiness, joy, abundance, security, right action, or divine love. You cannot determine exactly all of the events, circumstances, and experiences through which you will pass in your life's journey.

Unforeseen cataclysms, floods, earthquakes, typhoons, monsoons take place, which may destroy cities and properties, wiping out the holdings of thousands of people. Occasionally, you read about floods where cattle are drowned, people are drowned, and so on. Wars, insurrections, political upheavals take place from time to time. Like the war in Beirut. People are killing each other, buildings are being burned, and so on. The wise, of course, have to move out of there. The wise ones moved out of there before they saw all the trouble that is going on now. In other words, they were led by intuition. They were led by guidance and right action. Thousands of them fled to Athens and other places because they saw what was coming, and you can be protected that way, too.

These unforeseen political upheavals have unpredictable effects on currency and real estate. International tragedies and fear of war have had catastrophic effects on the stock markets of the world. All material possessions are vulnerable to change.

There is no real security in buildings or stocks or bonds or money in the bank. All of these are necessary, but there's no real security. The real security is your alignment with God. Say, "God is an ever-present help in times of trouble. God watches over me and cares for me."

For example, the value of a $10 bill depends upon the integrity and honesty of our government and its ability to back up a sound currency. A check from a bank or from another person really is only a piece of paper. Its value depends upon the honesty and integrity of the writer of the check and on your faith in the soundness of the bank.

When you invest in General Motors, AT&T, and other corporations, you're investing in the honesty, integrity, ability, and also the mental caliber of these men. You may win dividends, because you're investing in the honesty of these men, but also in their mental acumen, their sagacity, and the creative ideas which may bring fortunes to people.

If you devote some time and attention every day to scientific prayer and meditation, you will experience a changed mental attitude, and you cannot and will not suffer from the many hazards and unforeseen catastrophes which are enumerated in newspapers from time to time.

Walk in the consciousness of God's eternal supply. Realize God is an ever-present help in times of trouble. God is your instant, everlasting supply of support, meeting all your needs, at all times, everywhere, which means anything you need spiritually, mentally, materially, or in any other way.

Know in your heart that the overshadowing presence is watching over you and your children, your loved ones, and all your ways. Remember that as long as you maintain a prosperity consciousness, you cannot suffer losses.

For example, if your oil well suddenly dried up, and this happened to be the channel through which your money came to you, the money need would automatically come to you from some other source. The amount you would receive would definitely be equal to the income you had previously derived from the oil well.

When you build into your mentality the awareness of the eternal source of supply, you cannot become impoverished, and no matter what form wealth takes, you will always be amply supplied. It will be pressed down, shaken together, and running over. It will be pressed into your hands.

· · ·

Emerson said, "Nothing can bring you peace but the triumph of principles." A principle is the way a thing works. For example, water flows downhill. It expands when frozen. It takes the shape of any vessel in which it is poured. In your mind, when you think good, good follows; when you think evil, evil follows. Therefore, you have to learn how to navigate the waters of your mind.

When you learn the laws of life and practice them, you will develop a sense of security. There is the universal law of action and reaction. If you think, for example, of harmony, peace, beauty, right action, abundance, divine guidance, these thoughts form the matrix through which the healing power will flow.

Whatever is impressed in your subconscious mind is expressed as form, function, events, conditions. The inside governs the outside. It's not the other way around, for your inner mood, thought and feeling, control your destiny. When you build an airplane or an automobile, or when the engineer builds a bridge, he conforms to universal principles.

Yes, he's a profound student of the laws of mathematics, of stress and strain, and he's able to measure all these things. He takes into consideration the velocity of the wind, the weight of the train that will go over the bridge, and so on. All this is computed mathematically and scientifically, and he builds the bridge according to universal laws. Of course he's praying, because he's conforming to universal laws and principles.

The wheels of your car have to be round, otherwise you would be in trouble, wouldn't you? Would you build a flywheel off-center? No, you wouldn't. You could not navigate a ship unless learn the laws of navigation.

How about navigating your mind? Look at the engineer building that bridge. Doesn't he operate on the principle of mathematics? He has vision, too. He knows what he's doing and why he's doing it. In other words, the man who flies a plane learns the principles of aerial navigation. He studies, he applies these things, and when you get on the plane, you have faith and confidence in the navigator.

Some years ago I spoke to Taniguchi in Tokyo. They have about six million truth students there. They call it the *Seicho-No-Ie* movement, which means the home or the house of infinite life. Infinite life, of course, means God, the way God works.

Taniguchi told me that when the floods touch certain cities in Japan, the truth students are never there. "Oft times," he said, "the truth center where they meet and pray is not touched by the flood." These men believe they're always divinely guided and watched over by an overshadowing presence.

One of the teachers told me he went by boat to another city in Japan. When he arrived at the place to embark, he was an hour late because his watch had stopped. That ship was lost in a storm.

He believed that God was his guide and protector watching over him in all ways. His prayer was, "*God is guiding me in all my ways and watches over me. He's a lamp upon my feet and a light upon my path.*" That's a wonderful way to travel, isn't it?

Many people when they get on a plane or they're going by car say, "*Divine love goes before me today making stray joyous and glorious my way. The Lord, He it is that doth go before me wither so ever I goest. Behold, I send my messenger before my face to prepare the way.*"

The messengers are thoughts of love, peace, harmony, right action, and beauty. Let these messengers go before you when you take a trip, whether it's by boat or by air or by land. The messengers will go before you making straight and happy your way.

"The Lord he it is that doth go before thee, the Lordly power." There's only one presence and power, it's divine love going before you. Divine love surrounds you and enfolds you and enwraps you. It walks and talks in you.

Today we have Social Security. We have Medicare, pension checks, food stamps. Yes, we have spent billions of dollars. I think this is the most generous nation on the face of the earth, the largess of this nation is beyond imagination.

To hear people criticizing it, people born here, is fantastic. All you can say is that they're terribly ignorant. You have compassion for them, for they don't know any better. This country has given billions, poured out by our government all over the world for friends and so-called foes. Yet there is a deep sense of insecurity. There's apprehension and fear. There's talk of nuclear war, destruction, and talk of missiles and bombing and so forth.

In Hollywood and elsewhere, we see a pornographic cesspool of iniquity. Yes, we're aware of moral decay, swingers making a mockery of marriage, others saying we're living together without it. People are afraid to go out at night and walk the streets. Yes, there is a great sense of insecurity. Coddling of criminals, of course, is quite prevalent. Some of them are walking the street because of technicalities in the law. We speak of soft judges and that sort of thing, we're all familiar with it. Women are afraid to go out at night in larger cities of the country.

You might say, "What will I do?" You can write to local legislators, to your congressmen, to your councilmen, senators, tell them how you feel. Write a constructive letter. Point out the way things ought to be according to the Golden Rule and the law of love and say, "What are you going to do about it? You're our legislator." They'll pay attention to you.

Pray that infinite spirit in its wisdom selects men and women for government positions at all levels, city, state, and federal, who are spiritual and dedicated, who have a reverence for things divine, for we don't want any other person to represent us.

This will help. If we had enough people here in our own country who knew how to consistently pray scientifically, we would have a different congress. We'd have a different government on all levels.

We're told venereal disease is rampant among young people. Some of the doctors are shocked by its prevalence among teenagers. Heart disease and cancer and alcoholism are taking their toll, too. Some say the world is going to the dogs. But they said that in the days of Socrates, too.

No, the world isn't going to the dogs. It's going to God. There's no other place to go, for God is, and all there is. God is the living spirit within and the ground you walk on, the air you breathe. All is of God, for it is omnipresent, present everywhere. It must be present in you, must be present in the other fellow, everywhere.

If you take the wings of the morning and fly to the outermost parts of the sea, *"There shall thy hand lead me, and thy right hand shall hold me."* This is the eminence of the divine. "The eminent God and the transcendent God are one," as Emerson said, for there's only the one presence and the one power.

That's why the greatest of all truths says, *"Here, O Israel, the Lord thy God is one Lord."* *Israel* means a prince ruling with God, as was said 2,000 years ago. It means any person who recognizes the sovereignty of the spirit and the regnancy of his own thought, one who refuses to give power to any other presence. Such a person is an Israelite, and you're told that against an Israelite, not even a dog will lift its tongue.

There's no divination or enchantment against Israel, meaning against the man who walks with God and recognizes the one presence, the one power. For one with God is a majority, and if God be for you, who on earth can be against you?

No good thing shall be withheld from him who walks uprightly in the law. Realize, therefore, that God indwells you, walks, and talks in you. Read the 91st Psalm at night. Peruse it slowly, quietly, lovingly. Let it sink into your mind. Gradually you'll build up an immunity to all fear. You're told angels shall watch over you, meaning God's creative ideas. Inspiration will guide you, and divine love will surround you.

Read the 27th Psalm in the morning, the greatest antidote to fear in the world today. Saturate your mind with these truths. Charge your mental and spiritual batteries with these eternal truths that have stood the test of time for thousands of years, and as you do, you will become a broadcasting station, neutralizing to some degree the toxic effluvia of the mass mind.

The mass mind is what Judge Stewart called the law of averages, four billion people thinking, and you know very well too many of them are not thinking whatsoever things that are lovely, true, noble, and Godlike. Most of it is very negative, full of envy and jealousy. They're thinking of murder, and of sickness and disease and fires and wars and all that sort of thing. Surely, there's some good in it, but most of it is frightfully negative.

If you don't do your own thinking, who's going to do it for you? Are you going to let the mass mind do it for you, or the law of averages? If there's any fear or worry in your thinking, you are not thinking at all. You're not. It's the mass mind thinking, and you making an awful mess of your life.

You are thinking when your thought is completely free from fear and worry. You are thinking when it's from the standpoint of eternal verities, eternal truths, which never change. You will be thinking like an engineer, from the standpoint of universal principles, for nothing will give you peace but the triumph of principles. Therefore you would think a right action, divine law and order, divine beauty, divine peace, and inspiration from on high.

You would think in whatsoever things are true, whatsoever things are just, and whatsoever things are lovely, things that are honest, things that are of good report. Then, you would be thinking.

•   •   •

I read recently where there is a swing back to the old virtues. One article said that young men and women were flocking back to the seminaries, studying the scriptures with a hunger and a thirst to serve people. That's a good sign. Nature abhors extremes, and when you go to one extreme it throws you back to the opposite. Many people are hurt when that happens.

You don't want to be a part of the mass mind, which means the thinking of four billion people in the world, whose thoughts are mostly negative, as I brought out. If you do not do your own thinking, then the law of averages moves in upon you and disturbs your life. The law of averages, the people of the mass mind, believe in sickness and disease, misfortune and accidents, and all sorts of negative things.

If you don't do your own thinking, you're saying, "I'm going to take what comes," which is a very foolish thing because you don't know what comes. You don't know what's in that mass mind. All sorts of disorders are there.

It is well known that nature abhors extremes. Notice how we have gone to extremes in sexual depravity, perversion of all kinds, on screen and stage, abhorrent and repulsive. Nature has no other way than to cause us to swing back to the opposite. Nature always seeks a balance. If there's an earthquake, you know very well nature seeks a balance. Again there's quietude, serenity, tranquility, and a balance.

If there's a great battle out in the field, a lot of blood spilled and bodies wasted, a few years later you see the poppies growing up on that field. You'd think nothing ever happened there. Nature always seeks a balance.

When you disabuse the laws of your life, perhaps you find yourself on a hospital cot. You might call it a nervous breakdown, but it is benign nature compelling you to get back on the beam, the beam of God's glory. For the God presence is forever seeking to express itself through you as harmony, beauty, love, peace, joy, vitality, and wholeness. Therefore, if you refuse to let it flow through you in that way, it has no alternative but to cause you to come back to it.

You have time then to contemplate on the cot, don't you? You have time to meditate and to reflect, and you begin to realize that it was your negative, destructive thinking that caused you to land on that hospital cot, because you've been sending discordant vibrations all over your system, and your subconscious mind had no alternative but to reproduce them after their kind. Then we give it a fancy name, we call it a nervous breakdown, or we call it anxiety, neurosis, and other words, which is nothing more or less than chronic worry or a nasty disposition.

Realize God loves you and cares for you. The peace of the Almighty God floods your mind, your heart, and your whole being for God is peace, and that river of peace is flowing through you now, this very moment.

We said that nature abhors extremes, which it does. We had the old Victorian taboos and strictures.

Then came a violent swing to the opposite. We had the Freudian era, with its emphasis on sex followed by looseness, immorality, and aberrations of all kinds. Some people began to think that all the problems that we had were due to sexual frustration or repression, all of which is absurd.

Change eternal is at the root of all things. *"Change and decay all around I see, O thou who changest not, abide with me."* There is that within you that never changes. It's the same yesterday, today, and forever. Yet, change is constantly going on. It's the most unmovable of all, yet it's behind all movement. It's the omni-action of the infinite.

· · ·

Every day you read about wars and cataclysms and strife, ambushes, civil war, bombings of buildings, kidnappings, and so forth, all over the world. Ask yourself, "What can I do about this? How can I retain peace in this changing world?"

You can feel secure and retain peace, tranquility, serenity, and equanimity—yes you can. You can tune in with the infinite because it is written, *"Acquaint thyself with Him and be at peace, and good shall come to thee. With mine eyes stayed on God there is no evil on my pathway. Thou will keep him in perfect peace whose mind is stayed on thee because he trusteth in thee."*

Tune in with the infinite, which lies stretched in smiling repose. It is the primal cause. Divine love fills my soul, divine peace saturates my mind and my heart. The light of God enfolds me, and I am inspired from an eye.

The Bible tells you turn your eyes to the hills from whence cometh your help. You know very well the hills are of an inner reign. It represents the presence and power of the infinite within you which knows only the answer, for it is the finite alone which hath rotted and suffered. The infinite lies stretched in smiling repose.

That's the peace that passeth all understanding, for the center of your being is peace, and this is the peace of God. In this stillness you'll find strength, guidance, and love of the divine presence.

You know how the masses think. They're always going from one extreme to the other. One day it's war, and the next day it's a modicum of peace for a while. When these violent swings take place, many are hurt except those who tune in with the infinite and dwell in the secret place of the most high. You're told to come out from them and be separate. Come out from that mass mind and begin to think for yourself from a standpoint of the eternal verities and the great eternal truths of God. Come out from the mass mind, from the law of averages, and do your own thinking. Keep prayer up, and you won't suffer like the masses do.

When the flu comes, well you won't get it because you don't believe in it. You'll realize that the spirit in you can't be sick, frustrated. It can't be hurt or wounded, vitiated. It's the living spirit Almighty. It's omnipotent and supreme.

That's the reality of you, and by dwelling on that simple truth, you build up an immunity. You become God intoxicated. You have received the divine antibody, but if you're in the law of averages when the flu comes, they all get it. You don't want to live by the law of averages. The masses believe in sickness and misfortune, crime and poverty, accidents, jealousy, envy, all these are rampant in the mass mind.

Believe in the goodness of God and the guidance of God and the abundance of God in the land of the living. What do you believe in? Done unto as you believe, the way you believe. Begin to use divine principles in the same way a chemist uses the principles of chemistry, which are dependable. Surely he can use the principle two ways. He can make nitroglycerin, or he can also make nitroglycerin trinitrine tablets for the heart, which can save a human life.

How do you use it? He brings forth marvelous compounds which bless humanity because he wants to use the principle of chemistry wisely, constructively, judiciously. But you can also use the principles of chemistry to poison people and blow up a house, or a mine, or anything else.

* * *

Recently, the newspaper reported a fire in a nightclub. Many were trampled to death and burned to death. The article continued to say that there was no need for this panic at all. A fear seized the people, they became irrational. They lost their heads, so to speak, lost all reason. There were plenty of exits. Yet there were several there who remained quiet and calm, and nothing happened to them. They remained serene; they saw their way out. *"In quietness and in confidence shall be your strength."* Yes, divine law and order governs your life, and when divine law and order governs your life, you're always in your true place doing what you love to do, divinely happy and divinely prospered.

Fill your mind with eternal verities. Identify with the spirit within you. Or if you don't, or you just assume that you'll take what comes, that you can't be bothered, you're too lazy or apathetic or listless or indifferent, then you must not be surprised when reverses come, or setbacks or illness, and you say, "Why do these things happen to me? I'm so good."

You might say, like Job of old, that you're so good. You go to church, you give to the poor, and you sing hymns, you count your beads. There's nothing wrong with any of that, not a thing, and you pay your taxes, and you go to church every morning. Nothing wrong with it, but it's the thinking in your heart that matters.

It's what you really believe deep down in your heart. It's your emotional espousals. It's your deep convictions. It's your belief. You can do all these wonderful things externally, but if you have any fear or hate or resentment or condemnation or criticism or holier-than-thou attitude, looking at others and feeling sorry for them, or resentful towards them because they don't believe the way you do, or you're critical of them or you're full of fault-finding because that's unfortunate they don't believe the way you do, all these things bring on illness and sickness.

That's why the ancients had a saying, "Saints are all right in Heaven, but they're Hell on earth." Meaning these do-gooders, holier-than-thou, I'm-so-pious, and I'm-so-good people. "I'm better than all other men, look at what I do externally." But that's not the point.

It's how you're thinking and feeling in your heart, for as a man thinketh in his heart, so is he, so does he experience, so does he become. Your heart is your subjective mind. So if there's any resentment or condemnation there, or if you're angry, or if you're full of ill will and bitterness, or you're jealous of other people, these are poisons, and they pollute the soul. They bring on all manner of diseases, just like worry will bring on ulcers. Jealousy may affect your eyes and your liver, and anger can affect your blood pressure.

Yes, you can follow all the rules and the tenets of your church, regardless of what it is, and be very good from a conventional standpoint and still suffer the tortures within, because it is the belief in the heart that matters. The feeling, the emotional nature, your espousals, your convictions. That's the inner life, not the external thing. Many people suffer these setbacks and say, "Why should this happen to me—I'm so holy, I'm so good?"

You can build up an immunity, whereby you can't be hurt, sick, or defeated, because you practice the presence of God, and you realize that God walks and talks in you. God is guiding you. There is right action in your life, divine order in your life. God is your boss. God loves you and cares for you, and you're sold on that idea.

If there's fear and worry in your thinking, you are not thinking at all. Remember it's the law of averages thinking in you. So begin to think on whatsoever things are true and lovely and noble and God-like. Have ideas in your mind which heal, bless, inspire, elevate, and dignify your soul. Pour out goodwill to others. Radiate it to all men.

There's only one religion in the world, and that's a reverence for the God presence within. You're bound to a God of love, a God of peace, a God of joy, a God of happiness, a God of abundance, for I'm come with the man of life and have it more abundantly. If you're bound to that, isn't that a wonderful religion? Of course it is.

•   •   •

In one of our recent seminars in the sea, I saw a woman read the minds of about ten strangers. They were passengers on the ship. She never saw them before. She was about ninety percent accurate, according to these passengers.

Likewise, all of you are familiar with the work of Dr. Ryan, Duke University, also Professor Hartman, where they demonstrated clairvoyance, clairaudience, telekinesis, retro-cognition, precognition, prescience, and all these faculties of the mind.

Dr. Ryan's wife took 3,000 cases of precognition, dreams, visions of the night, and other extraordinary instances of extrasensory perception. These are all faculties that are within us, and perhaps ninety percent of the contents of your mind can be read by a good medium or clairvoyant. But they may see some negative things such as reverses or sickness or things of that nature, because the thought and the thing are one in the mind.

That's why you sometimes have a precognition in a dream. You've seen an event before it has happened, but it has already happened in your mind, for you see the thought of, say, a divorce in the divorce. That means it has already happened in your mind and can be seen by a good psychic.

If they saw reverses or accidents or losses or illness and things like that, they are simply tapping your subconscious. They get into a passive, psychic state, and they read your mind. You'll actually tell them everything before they tell you anything, simply tapping your deeper mind. Remember the thought and the thing are one in your mind.

If you're traveling to Europe, that travel has already taken place in your mind and can be seen. So what's strange about a good sensitive or a psychic saying you're taking a trip, you're going to Europe? It's already in your mind, isn't it? There is no mystery.

You can change your mind through scientific prayer, which means you can think from the standpoint of universal principles. You can think of divine right action, divine love, divine harmony, divine law and order governing your life, divine beauty, divine guidance, and divine love surrounding you, and the peace of the everlasting God flooding your mind, your heart, and your whole being.

As you change your mind, you've changed your body and your experiences, and you prevent these things from happening because you've transformed your mind. Therefore these negative things that would happen had you not prayed will not happen, because you changed your mind. As you change, attitude changes everything. As you fill your mind with the truths of God, you crowd out of your mind everything unlike God. A new beginning is a new end.

You prevent the reverses that she spoke of, or that were seen in your mind, prevent them from happening. Your avoidance of the negative pattern in your subconscious will depend on your spiritual awareness and the enlargement of your own consciousness.

As a woman told me the other day, "For three nights in succession I dreamt I saw myself having an accident driving to Pomona. I had an appointment in Pomona on Thursday, and Monday, Tuesday, and Wednesday, I dreamt of that accident. I didn't go to Pomona."

A woman asked her to join her on the trip to Pomona, and she didn't go. She told her why, and the woman said, "Well, that's only a dream." She said, "I know, but it's more than a dream to me."

This other woman had the accident on the way to Pomona. Had the first woman gone, she would probably have experienced it also, but she saw it in a dream and was asking for guidance and right action and didn't go. The other woman had invited her along, as they both had an appointment there, and she was wise not to go.

As you ascend spiritually, you would avoid the negative experiences of the mass mind. Extremes reverse themselves. Notice when people go too far to any extreme, they're violently thrown back to the opposite, aren't they? All of us are in the law of averages or mass mind. All of us are immersed in that mind, which is common to all men, and there are four billion people thinking into it. Stewart called it the law of averages, but by reiterating the truths of life and charging your mental and spiritual batteries regularly, systematically, we neutralize the toxins of the mass mind to a great extent.

If you allow your mind to be hypnotized or thought into by negative newscasters and by suggestions of doom and gloom, then these thoughts will govern you negatively and destructively as they become subjectified.

Prayer is the contemplation of the truths of God from the highest standpoint, and you are what you contemplate. You are what you think all day long. The Bible says, *"The Kingdom of Heaven is like unto a man which sowed good seed into his field, but while men slept,"* meaning they weren't vigilant, they weren't on the lookout, they weren't on alert, they weren't on the beam, they were lazy, they wouldn't bother praying. *"His enemy came and sowed tears among the wheat and went his way."* That's in the Book of Matthew.

The good seed represents your good thoughts and good ideas, thoughts which are lovely and of good report. When you are apathetic, listless, lazy, and indifferent, seeds of negative thoughts, of the mass mind, enter your mind, because all of us are subject to the suggestions of the mass mind.

You have to be constantly alert, on the beam of God's glory. You have to be vigilant at all times, constantly cremating the negative thoughts which bombard you silently and audibly. You don't want to be mesmerized and manipulated by the mass mind. Keep saturating your mind with God's ideas. There will be no room for the negative suggestions of others to enter.

Your subconscious responds to the convictions held by your conscious mind. You must really believe what you affirm. Longing to believe is not enough. One woman was saying, "God is the only presence and power. God is the only cause. God is the only substance. God is all there is in all, over all, through all, all in all."

That's all true, yet she was afraid of someone who she said was practicing voodoo against her. She was terrified—she didn't believe that God is all there is.

Her words were pure verbalisms, I call it frothing at the mouth.

I told her what Judge Stewart said when the people asked him, "What would you do if the black magicians were praying against you using the death prayer?"

"I would say cock-a-doodle-doo," he said, which means to laugh at the whole thing, because the suggestions of ignorant people have no power, except you give it power by accepting these suggestions. But the God presence, the spirit is the power. It moves as unity and harmony.

When your thoughts are God's thoughts, God's power is with your thoughts of good. That's why one with God is a majority. Of course Stewart was right. "I'd say cock-a-doodle-doo." You'd just laugh at it, they have no power.

It boomerangs because you don't receive it, boomerangs back to them. You don't give power to people who tell you you're going to fail, do you? You know you're born to win, to succeed. The infinite can't fail. It's a stimulus to your belief in your own success, in your own power of achievement, of accomplishment, of triumph.

The power is the spirit within. That's where the power is. It's one and indivisible. There's nothing to oppose it or challenge it. As you change your mind, you will neutralize any tragic event that may be registered in your subconscious mind. The 91st Psalm says, *"No evil shall befall thee or no plague shall come nigh thy dwelling."*

. . .

The late Walter Lanyon told me he took a taxi one time in Bombay, India. It was late at night, and he realized that when he got into the car, this man wasn't a taxi driver, but he looked like one, and the car looked like a taxi. It had the same color. He said he began to realize the presence of God where that man was, and the light of God was shining in him. The presence of God was there.

The man said to him when he drove him to the hotel, "You know, I was going to rob you, but somehow I couldn't." Lanyon told him why he couldn't, and gave him some pamphlets. He became a listener while he was lecturing in India. This man became a listener, in other words, he became transformed. It's possible for another person to tune in on your consciousness and be transformed.

The Bible says that people can't take up serpents, shall not touch them. Well, that depends upon a very high state of consciousness. In India people take serpents, put them around their necks, but the average man shouldn't do that. He's not at that level of consciousness.

If you're at a high state of consciousness, you can use a tiger as a pillow. Lao-Tze, of course, discovered that in 600 B.C. He went into the forest and there was no place for the fangs of the tiger or for any other animal to touch him, because he walked in the consciousness of God's love. He was at that high state of consciousness.

Animals sense fear. It's the scent of fear, and they pick it up, and they attack you. All animals pick up on your fear.

"*A thousand shall fall at thy side and 10,000 at thy right hand, shall not come nigh thee.*" As you walk in the light and consciousness of love and light and truth, you will extend yourself in all directions. You'll be immunized against all harm.

We suffer because we misuse the law. We deviate from the divine norm, which is harmony, love, and goodwill. It's natural to be healthy; it's abnormal to be sick. If we refuse to use the law righteously, then we shall have to suffer until we awaken to the truth.

Program your subconscious in the right way. You'll find a cassette there, programming your subconscious, a one-hour cassette. It's immensely popular. I recommend it to you. Program your subconscious in the right way. Or do you want the world with its false beliefs, false doctrines, and false philosophy to brainwash you and program you negatively?

You are a spiritual and also a biological being. There are two ends of the stick, as Stewart said. Don't deny the physical. You need a body to express. Every spirit builds itself a house. You are a temple of the living God.

How would you show what love was except you had a body? You're not an airy nothing. How would you play music? You can use your fingers to play the melody of God.

There are so-called pious people who look down at those who don't believe the way they do. They follow tenets and rituals blindly. They feel self-righteous, and when they suffer sickness or things go wrong, they get angry. They get mad at God, too.

All this is foolish because religion is of the heart, not of the lips, and when you condemn others, you're condemning yourself, and if you look down your nose at somebody because he doesn't believe in your creed, you're in for trouble, trouble you're making for yourself. For ill will brings on sickness, self-condemnation, self-criticism, or criticism of others.

It brings on all manner of illness and lack, loss and limitation. These negative attitudes are false pride, bringing on illness and neurosis and all manner of trouble. Some people are so good, they're good for nothing. So be bound to the one who forever is. Be bound to love. Get a God of love enthroned in your mind.

. . .

You have read about Saint Francis, Saint Augustine, and others, of course. Saint Augustine said, "Oh, Lord, give me chastity," and then he thought for a minute and said, "Oh, not yet."

Saint Francis was kind of a wild man, wasn't he? He had attended drunken orgies, and he was a sensualist and so forth. Many saints were libertines and profligates, but these people had a violent swing to the opposite extreme. They engaged in rigidities, austerities, began to fast.

Saint Francis used to beat his body. Late in life, he said, "Too late have I beaten my brother." His brother was his body, and he used to beat it. He thought it was evil, so he went to extremes.

Extremes are always bad. They're always dangerous. Nature, as I said, abhors extremes. He and others were zealots, and they overreacted. They went to the opposite and then began to punish themselves.

Look at all the problems of the world and realize one with God is the majority, and if God be for you, who can be against you? Cleanse your mind with the great eternal truths of God. Go through the happy medium. Don't go too far to the right or too far to the left. It's the middle road of Buddha, the straight and narrow gait of Jesus.

Walk in the light and realize divine love goes before you, making straight and beautiful your way. Realize the love, the light, and the glory of the infinite animates and sustains you. Realize that God is, *"thou will keep Him in perfect peace whose mind is stayed on thee."*

There is a prescription, a spiritual prescription, which enables you to find peace and strength and assurance. "Nothing happens to any man, that he is not formed by nature to bear," the philosopher said.

In Hawaii, a guide will show you a hut where the great writer, Robert Louis Stevenson, wrote his masterpiece *Treasure Island,* despite the fact that he was suffering from an acute case of tuberculosis. He felt secure in God. He tuned in on the infinite. There is a marvelous prescription for you, and it is this:

> "Thou will keep him in perfect peace whose mind is stayed on thee because he trusteth in thee." That's from Isaiah, the twenty-sixth chapter. Know that the inner desires of your heart come from God. God wants you to be happy. God's will for you is a greater measure of life, love, truth, and beauty. Mentally accept your good now. Become a perfect channel for the divine.

Realize you're an expression of God, that you're divinely directed in all your ways. You're always in your true place doing the thing you love to do, divinely happy and divinely prospered. Refuse to accept as truth the opinions of men.

Realize you're always reflecting divine wisdom and divine intelligence. God's ideas unfold within you, bring you harmony, health, and peace and joy. You're always poised, balanced, serene, and calm, for you know that God will always reveal to you the perfect solution to all your needs.

The Lord is your shepherd, and you shall not want for any good thing. You're divinely active and divinely creative. You sense and feel the rhythm of the divine. You hear the melody of God whispering its message of love to you. *"Come unto me all ye who labor and are heavy-laden, and I, the infinite, will give you rest."*

The Psalmist says, *"O, give thanks unto the Lord."* Call upon his name. Make known his deeds among the people. Sing unto him. Sing psalms unto him. Talk ye of all his wondrous works. Glory in His holy name that the heart of them rejoice that seek the Lord.

It says enter His gates with thanksgiving. Enter into His courts with praise. Be thankful unto Him, and bless His name, for the Lord, He is good. His mercy endureth for all generations, and the love, the light, and the glory of the infinite animates and sustains you.

"Come unto me all ye that labor and are heavy-laden, and I will give you a rest." God in the midst of you is

guiding you now. His peace fills your soul. You're always immersed in that holy omnipresence. You're bathed by the interior light, for it is written, *"I will lead the blind in a way they know not. I will lead them in paths they hath not known."*

Overcoming
Worry

Prolonged worry robs you of vitality, enthusiasm, and energy, and leaves you a physical and mental wreck. Psychosomatic doctors point out that chronic worry is behind numerous diseases such as asthma, allergies, cardiac trouble, high blood pressure, and a host of other illnesses too numerous to mention.

The worried mind is confused, divided, and is thinking aimlessly about a lot of things that are not true. Worry is really due to indolence, laziness, apathy, and indifference, because when a man or a woman wakes up, they don't have to think these types of thoughts. They can think of harmony, peace, beauty, right action, love, and understanding. Supplant the negative thought with the constructive thought.

Your problem is in your mind. You have a desire, the realization of which would solve your problem, but when you look at conditions and circumstances as they are, a negative thought comes to your mind, and your desire is in conflict with your fear. Your worry is your mind's acceptance of the negative conditions.

Realize that your desire is the gift of God. God is the living spirit within you. It's telling you to rise higher in life. It's also saying there is no power to challenge God, the living spirit within you, for there's only one power, not two or three or four. Just one. That power moves as unity, moves as harmony and peace. There are no divisions and quarrels in it, therefore, all you have to do is tune into the infinite and let the harmony and the peace and the love of the infinite flow through you.

Affirm to yourself, "God, or the supreme wisdom, gave me this desire. The Almighty power is now backing me up, revealing to me the perfect plan for its enfoldment, and I rest in that conviction." When worried thoughts come to your mind, remind yourself that infinite intelligence is bringing your desire, ideal, plan, or purpose, to pass in divine order. That's supplanting the negative thought. Continue on this attitude of mind and the day will break, and the shadows will flee away.

Some time ago, I interviewed a businessman whose doctor told him that there was nothing wrong with him physically but that he was suffering from anxiety neurosis. Anxiety neurosis is a $25 word for plain chronic worry, and the word *worry* when you translate it from its original root means to strangle, to choke, which is what man is doing to himself.

This man said to me, "Every time I pray or think about success, prosperity, and greater wealth, I start to worry about money, my business, and the future. It's wearing me down, and I am so tired." His vision of success and prosperity was thwarted by his chronic worry, and the fretting consumed his energy fruitlessly. It's like a leakage of electricity. If you have a short circuit, no light comes on.

The way he overcame his anxiety neurosis or worry was as follows. He began to have quiet sessions with himself, three or four times a day, when he declared solemnly, *"There is a spirit in man, and the inspiration of the Almighty giveth them understanding."* That's from Job.

"The Almighty power is within me, enabling me to be, to do, and to have. This wisdom and power of the Almighty backs me up and enables me to fulfill all my goals. I think about the wisdom and power of the Almighty regularly and systematically, and I no longer think about obstacles, delays, impediments, and failure. I know that thinking constantly along this line builds up my faith and confidence, and increases my strength and poise, for God hath not given us the spirit of fear, but of power and love and a sound mind."

As he continued to do this regularly and systematically, you know what happened: These truths entered into his conscious mind, and then the brain sent these healing vibrations all over his system. They went into his subconscious mind, and like spiritual penicillin, they destroyed the bacteria of worry, fear, anxiety, and all these negative thoughts.

In a month's time, he arrived in that awareness of strength, power, and intelligence, which were divinely implanted in him at his birth. He has conquered his worries by partaking in the spiritual medicine of the supreme wisdom and infinite intelligence locked in his subconscious depths.

• • •

About a year ago, a distraught mother visited me saying that she was terribly worried about her son in Vietnam. I gave her a specific prayer to use night and morning for herself and for her son. Subsequently, her son returned from Vietnam. He married and settled down, and she again came back to see me just as worried as before.

You see, she wasn't worried about the things she said she was worried about. She was just guilty of plain, downright laziness, apathy, indifference, and sloppy thinking, because all she had to do was to tune in on the infinite, which lay stretched in smiling repose, and think Godlike thoughts, and all the power of God would flow through these Godlike thoughts.

In other words, think good and good follows; think evil and evil follows. When your thoughts are God's thoughts, God's power is with your thoughts of good. It's as simple as that.

That's discipline. That's a cleansing of the mind like you clean out your own home and wash your windows. If you don't keep your house clean, all sorts of pestiferous insects come in, the paint falls off of the wall, and all manner of things begin to happen.

You have to keep cleaning the house, don't you? Well, the house is your mind. You have to keep constantly cleaning it, filling it with truths of God which crowd out of the mind everything unlike God.

She was worried during the second visit that her son may have married the wrong girl. She admitted that the girl was a wonderful wife, but she said, "All the time, I was so worried that their child might be born dead or crippled, but my daughter-in-law has given birth to a perfect child."

The mother was then worried about a money shortage in her son's home. This woman was not really worried about what she thought she was worried about. Her actual difficulty was that she had an inward sense of insecurity, she was emotionally immature, and certainly spiritually immature. If she were spiritually mature, she would have sat down and blessed her son and the daughter, realizing God was guiding them. There was right action in their lives and divine law and order governed them. Divine peace filled their soul and God was prospering them beyond their fondest dreams. How then could she be worried about them?

If you're worried about your son, your daughter, or your business, why don't you change that and say, "Why don't I bless my son, my daughter, my husband, my wife, my business? Why don't I pour out a benediction upon them? Why don't I claim what's true of God is true of them. Why don't I do it? Am I lazy, indolent, apathetic, listless? Am I a sloppy thinker? Do I have a dirty mind, or am I willing to do that which is right?"

If you are, and you're worried about your husband, you'll say, "My husband is God's man. The peace of God floods his mind. The love of God flows through him. He's divinely guided. Wherever he is, God is. He's in the sacred place of the most high, watched over by God and by God alone." How, then, could you be worried about your husband?

So, she was not worried about what she thought she was worried about. Her actual difficulty was that she has an inward sense of this insecurity, which I mentioned, and was not in tune with the infinite. With her own thought, she could get in tune with the infinite at any moment she wanted to. Isn't that laziness?

While talking to her, I was able to show her that she was the creator of her own worries. She thereupon replaced her inner sense of insecurity with a real feeling of security. I wrote out a special prayer for her to use.

• • •

How did you learn to walk? You made many attempts to walk across the floor, you fell down. You had a thought pattern, you began to move your legs and so forth. Gradually it became second nature when you walked across the floor. In other words, if you repeat a thought pattern and act over and over again, after a while it becomes second nature, which is the response of your subconscious mind to your conscious thinking, and acting. That's prayer, too.

I was in a drugstore in Detroit a few years ago. The pharmacist invited me to come behind the counter where he showed me a sign over the prescription department. "I will fear no evil for thou art with me." That's from the 23rd Psalm. He added that his store had been robbed by gangsters three times, and he had been held up twice with a gun pointed at his head. Following is the essence of his conversation:

"I think of that sentence, of the Psalm, and it falls as a blessing on my mind. I have taken this infinite presence and power within me as my partner, and I claim many times during the day the infinite intelligence within me is my higher self. It's my senior partner. This intelligence guides me and watches over me. His power and wisdom are instantly available to me. I am not alone. Now I feel secure because I know God's circle of love surrounds the store, myself, and all my customers. I will make this prayer a habit. I will fear no evil, for thou art with me. Thy rod and thy staff may comfort me. Goodness and mercy follow me all the days of my life, for I dwell in the house of God forever."

The house of God is your own mind. Your mind is where you walk and talk with God, for God is that supreme intelligence of boundless wisdom within you. It's locked in your own subconscious depths.

The pharmacist met the problem of anxiety and worry, and he overcame it. During the past four years, he's had no trouble and has prospered beyond his fondest dreams. He realized that his worry was irrational thought. It was due to downright laziness, and he became a straight-line thinker. Are you a straight-line thinker?

"*Behold I stand and knock at the door. If any man will hear my voice and open the door, I will come in and sup with him, and he with me.*" This is telling you that there's an infinite intelligence, a boundless wisdom which men call God, knocking at the door of your heart. It opens with an inside latch. All you have to do is let it in and contact it with your thought. It will lift you up, heal you, inspire you, guide you, and open for you new doors of expression and watch over and sustain you.

That's the presence and power that heals a cut on your finger, that if you burn yourself reduces the edema and gives you new skin and tissue. It's that which started your heartbeat and watches over you when you're sound asleep. It's just the same as if it weren't out there, except you use it. That's why I say worry is laziness.

A schoolteacher told me that the way she overcomes all her worries is to take her worries apart. She holds them up to the light of day to the light reason, dissects them, and cuts them up into small pieces. She's a smart schoolteacher. Then, she asks herself, "Are these real? Where do they come from? Do these worries have any power? Is there any principle behind them?" With her cool, rational thought, she dismembers her worries.

ABOUT THE AUTHOR

Born in 1898 on the southern coast of Ireland, JOSEPH MURPHY grew up in a large, devout Catholic family. Murphy's parents urged him to join the priesthood but as a young seminarian he found religious doctrine and catechism too limiting. Eager to peer more deeply into the internal mechanics of life, Murphy left seminary to dedicate his energies to chemistry, which he studied both before and after his religious training.

In the early 1920s, married yet still searching for his place in the world of career and commerce, Murphy relocated to America to seek employment as a chemist and druggist. After running a pharmacy counter at New York's Algonquin Hotel, Murphy renewed his study of mystical and metaphysical ideas. He read the works of Taoism, Confucianism, Transcendentalism, Buddhism, Scripture—and New Thought. The seeker grew fully enamored of the New Metaphysics sweeping the Western world. The causative power of thought, Murphy came to believe, revealed the authentic meaning of the world's religions, the deeper meaning of psychology, and the eternal laws of life.

In arriving at his matured spiritual outlook, Murphy told an interviewer that he studied in the 1930s with the same teacher who tutored his contemporary New Yorker and friend, mystic Neville Goddard (1905–1972). Murphy said they shared the same teacher: a turbaned man of black-Jewish descent named Abdullah.

In the late-1930s, Murphy began his climb as a minister and writer, soon lecturing on the radio and speaking live on both coasts. He wrote prolifically on the autosuggestive and causative faculties of thought, and reached a worldwide audience in 1963 in *The Power of Your Subconscious Mind*, which went on to sell millions of copies and has remained one of the most enduring books on positive-mind philosophy.

After career spanning dozens of books and thousands of lectures on positive-mind philosophy, Murphy died in 1981 in Laguna Hills, CA

JOSEPH MURPHY
TIMELINE

1898: Joseph Denis Murphy is born on May 20, the fourth of five children (three girls and two boys) to a devout Catholic family on the Southern Coast of Ireland in Ballydehob, County Cork. Murphy's father was headmaster of a local boys high school.

Circa 1914–1915: After being educated locally, Murphy studies chemistry in Dublin. Bowing to his parents' wishes he enrolls briefly in a Jesuit seminary. Dissatisfied with his studies, and unbelieving of the doctrine of no salvation outside the church, Murphy leaves seminary.

Circa 1916–1918: Murphy works as a pharmacist for England's Royal Army Medical Corps during World War I.

1918–1921: Murphy works as a pharmacist in Dublin. He earns a monthly salary of about $10.

1922: Dissatisfied with traditional religion and finding limited opportunities to practice as a chemist, Murphy just shy of age 24 arrives in New York City on April 17,

1922. He is accompanied by his wife, Madolyn, who is eight years his senior (wedding date unknown). He arrives with $23. Applies for citizenship in August.

1923–1938: Murphy works as a pharmacist in New York City including at a pharmacy counter at the Algonquin Hotel. He deepens his study into metaphysics and years later recounts having studied with the figure of Abdullah, a black man of Jewish descent whom Murphy's contemporary and fellow New Yorker, Neville Goddard (1905–1972), wrote that he studied with. Murphy reports that Abdullah tells Murphy that he actually had three brothers, not two. Upon checking with his mother, Murphy discovers that he had a third brother who died at birth and was never spoken of.

Circa 1931: Murphy begins attending the Church of the Healing Christ in New York City, presided over by Emmet Fox.

Circa 1938: Murphy is ordained as a Divine Science minster. He continues to work as a druggist and chemist.

1941: Murphy begins broadcasting metaphysical sermons over the radio.

1942: Murphy enlists as a pharmacist in the New York State National Guard, a post he holds until 1948.

1943: Murphy studies Tarot in New York City and comes to believe in symbolic correspondences between the Tarot cards and Scripture.

1945: Murphy writes his first book, *This Is It: The Art Of Metaphysical Demonstration.*

1946: Murphy is ordained as a Religious Science Minister in Los Angeles. He soon takes over the pulpit of the Institute for Religious Science in Rochester, New York. He publishes the short works *Wheels of Truth, The Perfect Answer,* and *Fear Not.*

1948: Murphy publishes *St. John Speaks, Love is Freedom,* and *The Twelve Powers Mystically Explained.*

1949: Murphy is re-ordained into Divine Science and becomes minister of the Los Angeles Divine Science Church, a post he will hold for the next 28 years. Services become so popular that they are held at the Wilshire Ebell Theater.

1952: Publishes *Riches Are Your Right.*

1953: Publishes *The Miracles of Your Mind, The Fragrance of God,* and *How to Use the Power of Prayer.*

1954: Publishes *The Magic of Faith* and *The Meaning of Reincarnation,* one of his most controversial books.

1955: Publishes *Believe in Yourself* and *How to Attract Money*, one of his most enduringly popular works.

1956: Murphy writes *Traveling With God* in which he recounts his international speaking tours, comparing New Thought with various global traditions. He also publishes *Peace Within Yourself* (*St. John Speaks* revised) and *Prayer Is the Answer*.

1957: Publishes *How to Use Your Healing Power*.

1958: Publishes the short works *Quiet Moments with God, Pray Your Way Through It, The Healing Power of Love, Stay Young Forever, Mental Poisons and Their Antidotes,* and *How to Pray With a Deck of Cards*.

1959: Publishes *Living Without Strain*.

1960: Publishes *Techniques in Prayer Therapy*.

1961: Publishes *You Can Change Your Whole Life* and *Nuclear Religion*.

1962: Publishes *Why Did This Happen to Me?*

1963: Publishes *The Power of Your Subconscious Mind*, which becomes a worldwide bestseller and a landmark of New Thought philosophy. The book's publication makes Murphy into one of the most widely known metaphysical writers in the world.

1964: Publishes *The Miracle of Mind Dynamics.*

1965: Publishes *The Amazing Laws of Cosmic Mind Power.*

1966: Publishes *Your Infinite Power to Be Rich.*

1968: Publishes *The Cosmic Power Within You.*

1969: Publishes *Infinite Power for Richer Living.*

1970: Publishes *Secrets of the I Ching.*

1971: Publishes *Psychic Perception: The Magic of Extra-sensory Perception.*

1972: Publishes *Miracle Power for Infinite Riches*

1973: Publishes *Telepsychics: The Magic Power of Perfect Living.*

1974: Publishes *The Cosmic Energizer: Miracle Power of the Universe.*

1976: Murphy's first wife Madolyn dies. He marries his secretary, Jean L. Murphy (nee Wright), also a Divine Science minister. He writes *Great Bible Truths for Human Problems.*

1977: Publishes *Within You Is the Power*

1979: Publishes *Songs of God*

1980: Publishes *How to Use the Laws of Mind*

1981: Murphy dies on December 16 in Laguna Hills, CA, where he and his wife Jean are living at the Leisure World retirement community, now known as Laguna Woods Village.

1982: *These Truths Can Change Your Life* is published posthumously.

1987: Canadian writer Bernard Cantin publishes the French language work *Joseph Murphy se raconte à Bernard Cantin* [*Joseph Murphy Speaks to Bernard Cantin*] with Quebec's Éditions Un Monde Différent. The book is based on an extended series of interviews Cantin conducted with Murphy before his death and provides a rare window into Murphy's career. It does not appear in English. *The Collected Essays of Joseph Murphy* is published posthumously.